30-SECOND
ARCHITECTURE

The 50 most significant principles
and styles in architecture, each
explained in half a minute

Editor
Edward Denison

Foreword by
Jonathan Glancey

Contributors
**Dragana Cebzan Antic
Nick Beech
Marjan Colletti
Edward Denison
Anne Hultzsch
David Littlefield
Steve Parnell**

METRO BOOKS
New York

METRO BOOK
New York

An Imprint of Sterling Publishing
1166 Avenue of the Americas
New York, NY 10036

This book was conceived,
designed, and produced by
Ivy Press
210 High Street, Lewes,
East Sussex BN7 2NS, U.K.
www.ivypress.co.uk

Creative Director Peter Bridgewater
Publisher Jason Hook
Editorial Director Caroline Earle
Art Director Michael Whitehead
Designer Ginny Zeal
Illustrator Ivan Hissey
Profiles Text Viv Croot
Glossaries Text Simon Smith
Project Editor Stephanie Evans

ISBN-13: 978-1-4351-6084-2

For information about custom
editions, special sales, and premium
and corporate purchases, please contact
Sterling Special Sales at 800-805-5489
or specialsales@sterlingpublishing.com.

Manufactured in China

Color origination by Ivy Press Reprographics

2 4 6 8 10 9 7 5 3 1

www.sterlingpublishing.com

CONTENTS

6 Foreword
8 Introduction

10 Foundations
12 GLOSSARY
14 Primitive/Vernacular
16 Ancient Egyptian
18 Classical Greek
20 Roman
22 Byzantine
24 Romanesque
26 **Profile: Vitruvius**
28 Gothic
30 Islamic

32 Key Innovations
34 GLOSSARY
36 The Arch
38 The Dome
40 The Vault
42 The Beam
44 **Profile: Palladio**
46 The Column
48 The Buttress
50 The Frame

52 Projection
54 GLOSSARY
56 The Plan
58 Section
60 Elevation
62 Symmetry
64 Perspective
66 Axonometric Projection
68 Scale
70 **Profile: Le Corbusier**

72 Theories/Concepts
74 GLOSSARY
76 Proportion & the Golden Ratio
78 Form Follows Function
80 Solid–Void
82 Less is More
84 **Profile: Louis Sullivan**
86 Aesthetics
88 Historicism
90 Paper Architecture
92 Critical Regionalism

94 Ideas/Movements
96 GLOSSARY
98 Classicism
100 The Renaissance
102 Revivalism
104 Arts & Crafts
106 Avant-garde
108 Modernism
110 Organic Architecture
112 **Profile: Frank Lloyd Wright**
114 Metabolism
116 High-tech
118 Postmodernism

120 Styles
122 GLOSSARY
124 Baroque
126 Orientalism
128 Art Nouveau
130 International Style
132 Art Deco
134 Brutalism
136 **Profile: I. M. Pei**

138 Future
140 GLOSSARY
142 CAD
144 **Profile: Richard Rogers**
146 Creative Reuse
148 Biomimetics
150 Sustainable Architecture

152 APPENDICES
154 Resources
156 Notes on Contributors
158 Index
160 Acknowledgments

FOREWORD
Jonathan Glancey

Architecture and building are almost but not quite one and the same thing. There would be no architecture without building, yet architecture attempts to raise the act of putting two bricks together well into the realms of Art. From the beginning of civilization, whether in the form of Sumerian ziggurats or Egyptian pyramids, architecture was a means of representing human dreams, hopes, and fears in three solid dimensions. A temple was always a more ambitious creative endeavor than a barn or cowshed, even if such agricultural buildings could be special things in their own right.

Ever since, architects have been a priesthood of sorts, shaping temples, whether to gods, God, Mammon, their patrons, and, in many cases, themselves. From the smallest house to the most ambitious museum or skyscraper, architects have been temple-builders. Indeed, in recent years, architecture has become as flamboyant as it ever was—partly because new materials and computer software allow architects to build wild dreams, but also because architecture itself remains such a powerful and visible expression of human vanity, aspiration, and ego. As for Imhotep, the first architect we know by name, he designed the first Egyptian pyramids and became a god; architects have thought highly of themselves ever since.

An edifice of ingenuity
The development of the dome during the Renaissance allowed for large, clear-span structures that were artistic and engineering masterpieces.

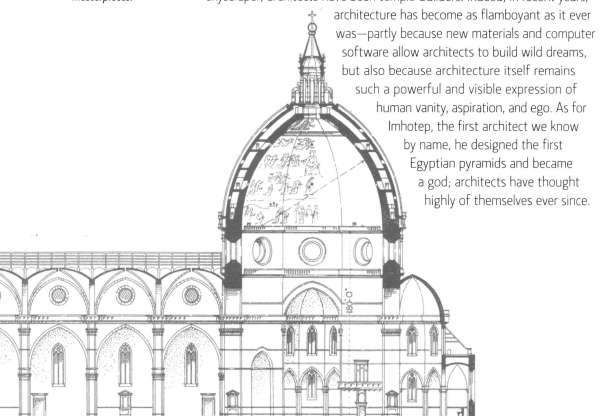

Architecture is an adventure. Buildings provide shelter and serve purposes, yet architecture has often pushed the limits of what such shelter might be. The Pantheon in Rome, one of the world's first great domed buildings, was nothing less than the Emperor Hadrian's model of the universe. The Gothic cathedrals of medieval Europe matched a sense of spiritual jubilation with bravura structural engineering and skilled masonry. Le Corbusier's soaring, numinous pilgrimage chapel at Ronchamp, consecrated in the mid-1950s, was a match for any ancient place of worship in terms of design and religious atmosphere. Babel-like skyscrapers continue to rise ever higher, pushing the boundaries of materials, design, engineering, and human daring.

Architecture has its own language, one that can be read in the façades of Greek temples, Georgian terraces, and Guggenheim museums. A building, a street, or an entire city center can be read like a book. The more you understand architecture, the richer a walk through any town or city becomes.

Not all architecture is sensational. And yet, in the many millions of quiet buildings designed by architects through the centuries, it is possible to detect something of the same intensity of design, and the will to create Art, found in the most ambitious temples. A modest Georgian terrace embodies the proportions and visual intelligence of the noblest Greek and Roman monuments.

However we choose to build in the future, and whatever our concerns about the environment, architecture will continue to play its role. We can build very quickly today and it would be easy to smother the planet in cheap and characterless buildings—and to an extent this is happening— but architecture is driven by dreams as much as by everyday concerns. Unlike building, it cannot be hurried. And, when we find a moment to stop and look up at a fine building, we see clearly just why architecture matters: it is our own human spirit, willed into stone and space.

INTRODUCTION
Edward Denison

Enduring forms
Greek and Roman architecture, that of their temples in particular, had in common many basic characteristics, among them the prominent portico and the column. The classical forms have proved enduring, reappearing in later architectural styles, from Baroque to Postmodernism.

Architecture is many things to many people. To some it is the ultimate art form, while to others it points toward science. But to many, it is simply about building or merely a matter of style. And in a digital age, to those more acquainted with constructing virtual worlds than real ones, architecture has nothing to do with buildings at all. Whatever our preconceptions, architecture is unique among art practices. First, it has to function and, second, it is particularly slow in its creation and appreciation.

It is ironic, then, that this slowest of arts should be given swift treatment here in 30-second portions. But this book attempts to explicate this unique artform through 50 key characteristics, from its origins in primitive building to its future in the virtual realm of advanced computer-aided design, or CAD. Each of the seven chapters concentrates on specific themes in architecture, exploring a wide range of topics across history, theory, and practice.

This journey starts with architecture's **Foundations**, when the time-honored practice of building, whether basic vernacular shelters or magnificent structures of stone, was transformed by the formal conventions of architecture prescribed by the Roman engineer and architectural primogenitor, Marcus Vitruvius Pollio. The structural elements that are fundamental to the development of architecture are the subject of the second section, which explains **Key Innovations**, including the arch, the beam, the column, as well as more advanced and complex structures such as the dome, the vault, and the frame.

The third and fourth sections explore fields of architectural theory and practice. Architectural representation is the focus of **Projection** in section three, which examines the significance of the plan, section, and elevation, as well as the notions of scale, symmetry, and perspective. Section four concentrates on key **Theories and Concepts** that have influenced the course of architecture, whether centuries-old, like the Golden Ratio, or more recent, like those that emerged from the Modern movement in the 20th century and consequent reactions to it.

Section five explores major architectural **Ideas and Movements** and fundamental ideas and events that have helped to shape them. Whether enduring, like Classicism, revolutionary, like Modernism, or transient, like Metabolism, architectural movements are distinctive for being uniquely influential not only in their lifetime and to their adherents, but also in their impact long after the movement has faded.

For those baffled by Baroque or Brutalism, section six offers a summary of the most significant architectural **Styles** in recent times. Every epoch has its own particular style and most buildings are dressed in a manner that reflects the period in which they were built, but occasionally these aesthetic considerations define the architecture, as occurred with the famously flamboyant Art Deco.

Looking to the **Future**, the final section examines how architecture is evolving and the challenges it faces. From notions of sustainability and biomimetics to the boundless potential of CAD, the future of this slow art promises change that is as rapid and unpredictable as has occurred at any time during its history.

Given that architecture, more than any other art form, shapes our world and how we interpret it, what is remarkable is that the discipline remains so ambiguous to many. In an attempt to demystify this often inscrutable subject, every entry in this book represents an important element of architecture and is presented consistently. Each one offers a "3-second foundation" that defines the topic in a single sentence, then a main text—"the 30-second architecture"—that explores the subject in detail, and a concluding "3-minute elevation" that places the topic in a wider context and offers further avenues of investigation.

These three different perspectives are intended to provide a practical and engaging introduction to each key topic that, read collectively, will paint a detailed picture of architecture and expose this enigmatic and omnipresent subject to a wide audience. *30-second Architecture* opens a window on our rich and exciting built environment.

Redefining the arch
The distinctive tip to New York's Chrysler Building has all the streamlined forms and stylized geometric shapes that characterize the glamorous Art Deco style.

FOUNDATIONS

FOUNDATIONS
GLOSSARY

architrave See entablature. Also refers to the molded frame surrounding a door or window.

central plan A type of plan that radiates out from a central point with roughly equal axes. This can range from a simple circle through the Greek-cross plan to any polygonal shape. It was common in church architecture in the Eastern Roman Empire and can be seen in the Hagia Sophia in Istanbul. A more recent example is Richard Rogers's Dome in London.

cornice See entablature. Also refers to any ornamental molding projecting outward from the top of a wall or other element of a building.

entablature The upper part of a Classical façade above a colonnade and beneath the pediment or roof. It is usually divided into three sections: the architrave (a beam or lintel immediately above the columns, ranging from plain in the Tuscan order to decorative in Ionic and Corinthian); the frieze (the middle section, which is often decorated with bas-relief sculptures); and the cornice (the top section immediately below the pediment or roof that projects out from the wall; it is usually decorated in bands that vary considerably between the orders).

fluting Usually refers to the shallow concave decorative grooves that run vertically up the shaft of a column, but they are also found on other surfaces.

flying buttress A buttress is any mass of masonry that is built against a wall to help counteract lateral forces from structures above, such as roofs. A flying buttress—a new development early in the Gothic period—makes use of an arch (full or half-width) to carry the thrust from the wall onto an external buttress or other support to channel it to the ground.

frieze See entablature. Also refers to any decorated band below a cornice on a wall.

groin The intersection where two vault roofs join.

lancet arch A pointed arch, in which the two radii of the arched section are longer than its width. A common feature of Gothic architecture.

micaceous mud Mud rich in fine-grained mineral-rich mica, particularly suitable for making strong sunbaked bricks.

oculus A small, circular, or oval window or opening in a wall or at the center of a dome.

orders The five orders of architecture are the accepted styles of Classical architecture that codified the decoration of the principal elements of a building, particularly the columns and entablature. The three ancient modes, originating in Greece, are Doric, Ionic, and Corinthian, and the Romans later added the plainest order, Tuscan, and the more elaborate Composite. The earliest surviving written description can be found in Vitruvius's *De Architectura* of c. 15 BCE.

pendentive A form of spandrel (broadly, the area between two arches) that allows a dome to sit on a square or polygonal structure. It does this by being concave in profile and, as it extends out from an angled joint of two walls, converts the angle to a curve.

pier A solid masonry support, more sturdy than a column, that ranges from a massive square-sectioned type to delicate composite piers found in Gothic structures. The term is also used to describe the area between windows and doors.

pronaos The vestibule of a Greek or Roman temple between the colonnade and the main building.

ribbed vault When barrel vaults intersect and the joins are decorated with piped masonry, a rib vault is formed—a development found in Gothic architecture in England.

stoa Either a covered colonnade (Greek) or a covered hall (Byzantine).

trabeated The term used to describe buildings constructed with columns and beams.

PRIMITIVE/ VERNACULAR

the 30-second architecture

3-SECOND FOUNDATION
Throughout history, most buildings have been the product of local building traditions working with materials at hand, rather than designed by architects.

3-MINUTE ELEVATION
Since Vitruvius in the 1st century BCE architects have written about the relationship between what we now call the vernacular and architecture. This is partly to distinguish one from the other, to argue that architecture is something distinct from simply building. But architects have also provided stories or myths about the origin of architecture in "primitive" building to prove that the architectural principles they defend are "true" because they are "natural."

"Vernacular" is a term used to distinguish the vast majority of buildings that are not designed by architects, but by individuals and communities who rely on long traditions of building from local materials. More diverse than any other type of architecture, the vernacular is evident in all parts of the world and throughout human history. As a category, it can include settler structures (such as huts, farmhouses, and towns) and nomadic structures (including dwellings made of canvas, hide, timber, and bone). Vernacular architecture closely reflects the cultural values of the people who build it. Often constructed from the same materials as the landscape in which it exists, it can be found standing on stilts by water, cut into rock, open in hot climates, insulated in cold climates. The most common vernacular architecture is domestic, but communal, sacred, commercial, and other built spaces can also be vernacular. Such architecture often uses simple methods to achieve sophisticated levels of comfort by controlling temperature (cooling or warming), air (drawing in fresh air and blowing out smoke and smells), and light (shade), and managing complex "programs" (the mixture of activities that go on inside the building).

RELATED TOPICS
See also
ARTS & CRAFTS
page 104

CRITICAL REGIONALISM
page 92

ORGANIC ARCHITECTURE
page 110

BIOMIMETICS
page 148

30-SECOND TEXT
Nick Beech

Vernacular architecture includes a wealth of building techniques and materials, applied to a wide variety of social and cultural ends.

ANCIENT EGYPTIAN

the 30-second architecture

RELATED TOPICS
See also
PRIMITIVE/VERNACULAR
page 14

CLASSICAL GREEK
page 18

ROMAN
page 20

REVIVALISM
page 102

ART DECO
page 132

3-SECOND FOUNDATION
The architecture of ancient Egypt encompassed a wide variety of types, from simple structures of sunbaked brick to monumental pyramids of dressed stone blocks.

3-MINUTE ELEVATION
The conditions in Egypt were ideal for monumental construction projects. Stone and sand were abundant and river transport easy, and with only one harvest a year the vast numbers of workers required to build the pyramids could spend half the year cultivating the land and half the year on the buildings. As a precedent for the Greeks and Romans, the architecture of ancient Egypt is regarded as one of the primary sources for Western architecture.

The ancient Egyptian civilization

lasted nearly three millennia, ending with Alexander the Great's arrival in 332 BCE. Early Egyptian construction was typical of many primitive societies, relying on locally abundant materials—in this case, timber, papyrus, and reeds. The Egyptians also mastered the manufacturing of sundried hard brick from the rich micaceous mud in the Nile delta that was mixed with sand and straw. Egyptian architecture will always be most famous for its monumental structures. These included palaces, temples such as the colonnaded funerary complex of Queen Hatshepsut (c. 1473–58 BCE), and the various pharaohs' tombs, better known as pyramids. The first pyramid was designed by the architect and engineer Imhotep, and built at Saqqara in c. 2630 BCE. Although the profile of this first pyramid was stepped, it set a precedent for later designs, the most famous of which are at Giza outside modern-day Cairo. The largest of these, built c. 2550 BCE for the pharaoh Khufu, rose to 481 ft and used over two million blocks of stone each weighing between 2 and 15 tons. It remained the tallest manmade structure on earth until Lincoln Cathedral in England was built in 1311.

3-SECOND BIOGRAPHIES
IMHOTEP
fl. 27th century BCE
Designer of the first stepped pyramid and one of the first people ever to be recorded as an architect (later deified)

30-SECOND TEXT
Edward Denison

The structures of ancient Egypt were an important precedent for the subsequent development of architecture in Europe.

CLASSICAL GREEK

the 30-second architecture

3-SECOND FOUNDATION
Classical Greek
architecture utilizes a
limited structural system
of columns and beams,
arranged according to
delicate geometries and
elaborately decorated.

3-MINUTE ELEVATION
The Greeks were
concerned with how
their buildings looked
and used optical illusions.
Their temples did not use
straight lines, since if a
beam were completely
straight it would appear
to sag, and a strictly
vertical column would
appear to lean outward.
Similarly, fluting makes
columns appear more
slender than plainer
columns. All that remains
of these temples is the
marble, but they were
once richly decorated and
painted with many colors.

Classical Greek architecture
(c. 500–320 BCE) seems familiar because many
of its features were subsequently revived and
reinvented. While banks, libraries, and museums
in Western cities use Classical Greek architecture
to inform their appearance, these mainly draw
on the temple or stoa (a covered arcade). Other
building types of Classical Greece include the
theater (a large bowl of steps and seats), the
hippodrome (a racing track), and the mausoleum
(tomb). Classical Greek architecture is trabeated,
which means it is constructed from vertical
posts (columns) supporting horizontal lintels
(beams). Originally of timber, in the transition to
stone these basic elements became increasingly
formalized and decorated. The spacing and
organization of the elements followed geometric
proportions designed to produce harmonious
relations between the parts. Lintels were divided
into horizontal sections: a plain architrave
below a frieze (decorated with relief carvings
celebrating historical and mythical events),
above that a projecting cornice. Columns were
fluted, and the top—the capital—was treated in
different ways, resulting in three distinct styles
or "orders" of Greek architecture: the Doric has
a plain capital; the Ionic has a capital carved to
form scrolls; and the Corinthian capital is carved
to resemble foliage.

RELATED TOPICS
See also
ROMAN
page 20

THE BEAM
page 42

THE COLUMN
page 46

3-SECOND BIOGRAPHIES
PHIDIAS
c. 480–30 BCE
Architect and sculptor of the
statue of Zeus at Olympia

ICTINUS
fl. late 5th century BCE
Architect of the Parthenon

DEINOCRATES OF RHODES
fl. mid-4th century BCE
Architect and city planner
of Alexandria

30-SECOND TEXT
Nick Beech

*For many European
architects, the Greek
temple—notably the
Parthenon in Athens—
represents the finest
achievement in
architecture.*

ROMAN

the 30-second architecture

Roman architecture borrows from the classical Greek, and can appear similar. However, during the period c. 200 BCE—CE 300, the Romans greatly advanced structural engineering, introducing the arch, vault, and dome, as well as a new material—concrete. These innovations affect the scale of Roman architecture because arches can support greater loads and span wider voids than trabeated structures. Massive freestanding edifices, of a size previously reliant on natural features such as hillsides (as in Greek theaters), could be built—famously the Colosseum in Rome, which was copied throughout the Roman Empire. New building types were introduced—baths with high-vaulted ceilings covering rooms and pools, massive basilicas (covered public spaces), palaces, and the triumphal arch. Unlike Greek temples, Roman temples were raised up on a high podium accessed by steps that terminate at the pronaos (a porch of columns), emphasizing one side of the building. A new Composite order was introduced, and concrete-and-brick buildings were decorated with extraordinary mosaics of tile. Still, the remains of Roman architecture that might impress us most today were the great public works, the aqueducts, tunnels, bridges, and roads that allowed Rome to become a city of one million residents.

3-SECOND FOUNDATION
Roman architecture developed from Classical Greek and introduced the arch, the dome, concrete, and mosaic tiles, and expanded the range of building types and their decoration.

3-MINUTE ELEVATION
As a result of their innovations the Romans had one architectural problem unknown to the Greeks—how to bring together straight, angular forms with curved forms. This dilemma is best demonstrated at the Parthenon (c. 126), where the glorious domed concrete roof with its oculus in the center—all held up by a massive drum—seems to bump into the linear columnar porch at the entrance.

RELATED TOPICS
See also
CLASSICAL GREEK
page 18

THE DOME
page 38

THE VAULT
page 40

3-SECOND BIOGRAPHIES
APOLLODORUS OF DAMASCUS
fl. 2nd century
Greek architect and engineer, designed Rome's Trajan Forum

30-SECOND TEXT
Nick Beech

Roman architecture is spectacular in two senses—in feats of engineering and in representing an empire of millions.

BYZANTINE

the 30-second architecture

3-SECOND FOUNDATION
An eclectic architecture, often utilizing the dome, which reflects the cultural diversity of the Byzantine Empire, centered on Constantinople from the 4th century.

3-MINUTE ELEVATION
Although the power and influence of Byzantium began to wane from the 11th century—eventually succumbing to the Turks in 1453—its architecture continued to influence builders throughout southern and eastern Europe. From Venice's St. Mark's Basilica (consecrated 1094) to Kiev's 11th-century St. Sophia Cathedral and beyond, the impact of the Byzantine plan and crowning dome is clearly visible on stone and wooden churches of different denominations and sizes throughout much of Europe.

The fragmentation of the Roman

Empire led to systemic collapse in Western Europe, but in the Eastern Roman Empire laws, customs, and building traditions were kept alive in the Byzantine Empire, centered on Constantinople (now Istanbul). This location led to the adoption of customs from the eastern Mediterranean, notably Greek culture and Christianity. The most common expression of architecture in the Byzantine Empire was in religious buildings, particularly churches. An exemplar of this architectural type was the Hagia Sophia (537), commissioned by Justinian I and designed by Isidore of Miletus and Anthemius of Tralles. In the center of the symmetrical plan rises a huge 107-ft diameter dome supported on pendentives that transfer the load onto four massive piers. The audacious design in an earthquake zone proved too daring, and the dome had to be rebuilt on several occasions. However, despite these misfortunes, Hagia Sophia set a benchmark in church construction and design for many centuries. One of the most prominent and enduring features of Byzantine church architecture, besides the use of the dome, was the central plan, based on the Roman temple and early Christian churches and the cruciform plan of Greek origin.

RELATED TOPICS
See also
CLASSICAL GREEK
page 18

ROMAN
page 20

ROMANESQUE
page 24

GOTHIC
page 28

3-SECOND BIOGRAPHIES
ISIDORE OF MILETUS
fl. mid-6th century
Byzantine architect, engineer, and mathematician who assisted in the design and construction of Hagia Sophia

ANTHEMIUS OF TRALLES
c. 474–before 558
Byzantine architect and geometrician, responsible for the design and construction of Hagia Sophia

30-SECOND TEXT
Edward Denison

The symmetrical plan and the dome are key characteristics of Byzantine architecture.

ROMANESQUE

the 30-second architecture

Romanesque architecture marked
the first time since the Roman Empire that a consistent architectural language appeared throughout much of Europe. It derived from Rome in so much as it often appropriated such features as round arches and vaulting, although Romanesque architecture was not a continuation of Roman practices and principles. Instead, it was a revival during the Holy Roman Empire of various architectural influences of the Mediterranean region. The first phase was typified during the reign of Emperor Otto I (962–73) and drew on Carolingian and Byzantine precedents, but its heyday was from the 10th to 12th centuries when some of the most advanced vaulting systems (barrel, dome, and groin) were constructed, stone was dressed, and elaborate details adorned buildings. Aesthetically, Romanesque architecture tends to be heavy, relying on thick load-bearing walls to support vaulted masonry roofs. Churches such as that at Cluny, France (dedicated 1130) were the most outstanding manifestations of the style, but it was also used in military installations and domestic buildings. Romanesque churches are characterized by symmetrical plans, solidity of form, fireproof masonry construction, vaulted roofs, round-arched openings, and, in larger structures, arcades of massive supporting columns and piers.

RELATED TOPICS
See also
ROMAN
page 20

BYZANTINE
page 22

GOTHIC
page 28

REVIVALISM
page 102

3-SECOND FOUNDATION
Romanesque architecture flourished throughout southern and western Europe from the 8th century, and is characterized by load-bearing masonry walls, round arches, narrow openings, arcades, and vaulting.

3-MINUTE ELEVATION
Experimentation by master builders and stonemasons, not scientific analysis, led to a steady refinement of construction techniques into the 12th century. The features that characterize Romanesque architecture were, ironically, also the attributes constraining its progress. The structurally inefficient round arch was replaced by the pointed arch, liberating the exterior walls from much of their load-bearing duties, and in time giving rise to the next great architectural epoch, Gothic.

3-SECOND BIOGRAPHIES
BUSCHETODI GIOVANNI GIUDICE
fl. late 11th century
Architect commissioned in 1063 to design the Santa Maria Assunta Cathedral, Pisa

30-SECOND TEXT
Edward Denison

Round arches, load-bearing masonry construction, dressed stone, and elaborate vaulting typify Romanesque design.

c. 80–70 BCE
Born in Rome

49–5 BCE
Great Roman Civil War (Caesar's Civil War), in which Vitruvius fought, possibly in the Legio VI Ferrata (the Sixth Ironclad Legion)

19 BCE
Completed work on a basilica at Fanum Fortunae (modern Fano)

c. 15 BCE
De Architectura (*Ten Books on Architecture*) written

after 15 BCE
Died

c. 800–25
De Architectura copied in manuscript at the Abbey of St. Pantaleon, Cologne, on the orders of the Holy Roman Emperor Charlemagne

1244
De Architectura quoted extensively by Vincent de Beauvais in his encyclopedia, *Speculum Maiu*

1414
Modern rediscovery of *De Architectura* by the Classical scholar Poggio Bracciolini

1443–52
Italian polymath Leon Battista Alberti writes *De Re Aedificatoria* (*On the Art of Building*) based on *De Architectura*

1486
First printed edition of Vitruvius in Rome, edited by Fra Giovanni Sulpitius

c. 1487
Leonardo da Vinci draws the "Vitruvian Man"

1511
First illustrated edition of *De Architectura* published in the Republic of Venice

1521
Italian edition published

1543
German translation published

1547
French translation published

1624
Sir Henry Wotton translates *De Architectura* into English

VITRUVIUS

Marcus Vitruvius Pollio was born in Rome. Best known today as an architect and writer, he considered himself first and foremost an army engineer and most probably served with the legendary Sixth Ironclad Legion, an artillery unit, where he was in charge of ballistics and siege engines.

Not much is known about Vitruvius—which may not even have been his name—and he was fairly obscure in his own time, although obviously valued in high places, being an essential part of Julius Caesar's battle team and granted a pension by Caesar Augustus in later life. He only made one actual building, a basilica in Fano that was finished toward the end of his life, and now untraceable, although it has probably been incorporated into the city's cathedral as happened to so many pre-Christian basilicas.

Vitruvius's great work was his writing, rather than his building. He compiled the 10-volume treatise *De Architectura* (usually translated as *Ten Books on Architecture*), written in Latin and Greek, and probably finished around 15 BCE. It is the only work on architecture from Classical antiquity to survive in its entirety and was intended as a building guide for his patron Augustus, the emperor who stated that he "found Rome brick and left it marble." *De Architectura* is extremely thorough, covering town planning, civil engineering, building materials, temples, the orders of architecture, civic building, domestic building, pavements and plasterwork, infrastructure (sewage, aqueducts, central heating), and the application of science to architecture and machinery.

A seminal influence on Renaissance, Baroque, and Neoclassical architecture, it was well known in manuscript, before being transcribed in the 9th century on the orders of the Emperor Charlemagne. It was read by scholars of all disciplines, including Aquinas, Petrarch, and Boccaccio, before being "rediscovered" in the 15th century and publicized by Leon Battista Alberti, who based his own 1452 opus, *De Re Aedificatoria*, on it. Architecture aside, it is also the principal source for the story of Archimedes's "*Eureka!*" moment.

It wasn't all measuring and materials, however. Vitruvius expressed his three virtues—the Vitruvian Triad of good building: *firmitas*, *utilitas*, *venustas* (solidity, usefulness, beauty)—and his belief that architecture should follow nature and that proportion in building should follow proportion in a human being. It was this that inspired Leonardo da Vinci to produce the "Vitruvian Man," essentially an infographic of the ideas of Vitruvius and an image that remains iconic today.

GOTHIC

the 30-second architecture

Gothic architecture emerged in Northern Europe during the Middle Ages, a period in which the Church dominated European cultural life—consequently, the finest examples of Gothic architecture are cathedrals and monasteries. Master stonemasons and their workshops produced buildings of great height that were also full of light. Based on elaborate practical geometry, Gothic architecture combines three key structural elements: the lancet (pointed) arch, which was able to hold a greater load than a rounded arch; this is combined with the ribbed vault, a system of vaulting that provides a ceiling that is higher, lighter, and able to join spans of different widths; and the flying buttress, a system of masonry blocks (the buttress), attached with arches to the exterior walls of the building, countering outward thrust from the high ceiling and walls. In combination, these three elements allowed for the replacement of thick walls with tracery, very thin stone patterns holding stained glass. Ecclesiastical buildings were highly decorated with biblical figures, gargoyles (gross monsters), animals, plants, and even pagan figures. As with the architecture of ancient Greece and Rome, many Gothic buildings are now bare stone when originally they were richly decorated with colored paintwork.

3-SECOND FOUNDATION
During the Middle Ages a new style of ecclesiastical building emerged in France that used pointed arches, ribbed vaults, and flying buttresses to extraordinary effect.

3-MINUTE ELEVATION
Gothic architecture creates unique experiences—a constant sense of movement as the eye follows the lines made by the ribs of the arches and vaults, a powerful lift upward, and extraordinary displays of light and color. These buildings were more than houses of God—through the stained glass and carved figures they were engines for the gathering and education of all members of European society.

RELATED TOPICS
See also
ROMANESQUE
page 24

THE VAULT
page 40

THE BUTTRESS
page 48

3-SECOND BIOGRAPHIES
ERHARD HEIDENREICH
c. 1470–1524
German master mason, best known for the vaulting at the Church of Our Lady of Ingolstadt, Bavaria

ABBOT SUGER
c. 1081–1151
French abbot of St. Denis (on the outskirts of Paris), who, from 1122, built the very first Gothic church

30-SECOND TEXT
Nick Beech

A Gothic cathedral is the product of tens, sometimes hundreds, of years of work and the combination of the skills and knowledge of many master craftsmen.

ISLAMIC

the 30-second architecture

Islamic architecture was born out of the rapid spread of Islam that followed the death of the Prophet Mohammed in 632. Initially, the architectural forms were influenced by regional precedents such as Byzantine architecture and often concentrated on religious structures, including mosques, shrines, and tombs. One of the earliest and most significant Islamic buildings is the Dome of the Rock (691) in Jerusalem. The central plan—defined by the octagonal exterior, concentric aisles, and central wooden dome—mirrors the contemporaneous centrally planned Byzantine churches. However, with the rapid spread of Islam throughout North Africa, southern Europe, and Central Asia, the architecture, like the Islamic religion and culture, became more assured and assumed distinctive characteristics, while also assimilating indigenous customs and traditions and accommodating local construction techniques. Islam's propagation also saw architecture being employed in secular buildings, such as palaces, civic structures, and the home. Despite Islam's extreme cultural, artistic, and regional diversity, common architectural features and principles include the precedence of geometry, the primacy of enclosed space and privacy (in the courtyard), and the abundant use of interior decoration to conceal the structural elements and convey weightlessness, magnificence, and beauty.

3-SECOND FOUNDATION
Islamic architecture originated in Arabia and spread with Islam from southern Spain across North Africa and the Middle East to Asia.

3-MINUTE ELEVATION
Islamic architecture is often referred to as the "architecture of the veil," suggesting that it is an art form devoted to concealment, a hidden architecture. This is apparent both in the design of a building and its place within a group of buildings or city. The exterior of Islamic buildings seldom reveal their function or the layout of the space within, and are often designed to blend in with their surroundings, rather than stand out.

RELATED TOPICS
See also
ROMAN
page 20

BYZANTINE
page 22

ROMANESQUE
page 24

GOTHIC
page 28

THE DOME
page 38

3-SECOND BIOGRAPHIES
MIMAR SINAN
1489–1588
Architect and civil engineer of the Ottoman Empire

USTAD AHMAD LAHAURI
d. 1649
Indian architect of Persian origin, associated with the design of the Taj Mahal

30-SECOND TEXT
Edward Denison

Islamic architecture often adopted local building precedents across Europe, Africa, and Asia.

KEY INNOVATIONS

arris The sharp edge formed where two surfaces meet.

balloon framing A timber-construction technique, in which long timber studs are assembled for the vertical elements first and the floors subsequently attached to these. Most commonly found in North America and Scandinavia.

caryatid A full (usually) female figure in place of a supporting column to hold up the entablature of a building. Male caryatids were also used—called atlantes—as well as three-quarter-length figures—herms—and other creatures, both mythical and actual.

catenary arch An arch like an upside-down catenary, the shape made when a chain or rope is allowed to hang under its own weight. The Gateway Arch, St. Louis, Missouri, is a classic example.

coffering Ceiling decoration that is made up of sunken panels, either square or polygonal.

compound dome A dome in which the pendentives beneath the dome proper form part of a larger sphere on which the dome sits. This is to be distinguished from a simple dome, where the pendentives are part of the same overall sphere as the actual dome.

ethylene tetrafluoroethylene ETFE is a polymer with a high resistance to the effects of weathering and other destructive forces. In architecture, it has been used as an outer skin for such high-profile projects as the Eden Project, Cornwall, UK, and the Beijing National Aquatics Center, China.

fan vault A vault where the decoration consists of fan-shaped cones of ribs that do not quite meet at the apex of the vault, so leaving a flat lozenge-shaped area. Most often found in English Gothic cathedrals.

geodesic dome This is a dome constructed from the triangular sections that are created when circles are drawn onto a sphere. They are very strong but lightweight structures that can be used to cover large areas.

inflexed arch In its simplest form, an arch in which the radii are inverted, or inflexed, such that they form a structure with a pointed apex curving down and out to the springer. These can sometimes have multiple points within the arch, but always with the curves facing into rather than out of the negative space.

parabolic arch An arch similar to a catenary arch formed out of a parabola. This is a very strong form that needs no extra support to take the forces exerted. First used in the late 19th century by the Spanish architect Antoni Gaudí.

piloti Columns or pillars that raise a building above ground level so leaving the street level open.

platform framing A form of timber construction in which—once the understructure is assembled—the upright elements are built on top of the platforms that make up the floors of each story. Much used in North America as a less labor-intensive form of construction than the more traditional balloon framing.

saucer dome A dome where the section is shallower than a semicircle. One modern example of this is the Louisiana Superdome, New Orleans.

"skin-and-bone" architecture A term used by Modernist architect Mies van der Rohe to describe his style of architecture, in which the "skin" of the walls is laid onto the "bone" of the frame of the building.

springer The section of an arch at the top of the uprights and from which the arch itself "springs."

tied arch Most often used for bridges, this is where the arched element of a structure is "tied" to the horizontal over which it spans to counteract the outward forces exerted on the arch.

voussoir A wedge-shaped stone or other tapered element of an arch.

wagon vault Alternative name for a tunnel vault, the most basic vault with no cross vaulting.

THE ARCH

the 30-second architecture

Ancient Greek stone architecture used a system of vertical columns and horizontal architraves. This type of structure originated in simple wooden constructions and did not allow for wide spans, which limited the scope of architectural possibilities. However, once the ancient Etruscans developed the first arches, the erection of much larger masonry structures such as bridges and aqueducts became possible. The arch was adopted by the Romans, who also built triumphal arches as monumental passageways to celebrate military victories. Arches have come in many forms and shapes over the centuries, including the Roman semicircular arch, the Gothic pointed arch and trefoil arch, the Moorish horseshoe multilobed arch, and the Baroque elliptical arch. There are also flat, tied, and inflexed arches, but the strongest are parabolic and catenary arches, introduced by Spanish architect Antoni Gaudí in the 19th century. Both parabolic and catenary arches are designed to carry all the downward forces into the ground without using buttresses or other supports. The arch continues to be a common architectural feature, and is still often used today for wide-span steel bridges.

3-SECOND FOUNDATION
An arch is a curved load-bearing structure that spans a void. Vertical forces are carried through the arch and into supporting abutments, called piers.

3-MINUTE ELEVATION
In a conventional arch, all the individual elements are arranged to create a closed system. The first stones above the supporting piers are the springers, which carry the wedge-shaped elements called voussoirs. The keystone at the apex of the arch completes the structure. However, depending on the curve, horizontal forces can push outward at the base. In Gothic cathedrals, for example, external elements—flying buttresses—counteract these forces, channeling them into the ground.

RELATED TOPICS
See also
ROMAN
page 20

ROMANESQUE
page 24

GOTHIC
page 28

THE DOME
page 38

THE VAULT
page 40

3-SECOND BIOGRAPHIES
EERO SAARINEN
1910–61
Finnish-American architect who erected the 630-ft Gateway Arch in St. Louis, Missouri

SANTIAGO CALATRAVA
1951–
Spanish architect/engineer who designs slim-dimensioned steel arched structures

30-SECOND TEXT
Marjan Colletti

Arches are very distinct features and, as such, an aid to recognizing the style of architecture.

THE DOME

the 30-second architecture

Simple domed structures of perishable materials such as wigwams and igloos date back to prehistoric times, but the dome proper was developed during the Roman Empire—and at 142 ft, the Pantheon in Rome (c. 126) is still the world's largest hemispherical, coffered, non-reinforced-concrete dome. Domes come in a multitude of different types and shapes: corbel domes (in the ancient Middle East), onion domes (in Russia, Turkey, the Middle East, and India), compound ones supported by pendentives such as the Hagia Sophia in Istanbul (537), spherical or part-spherical geodesic domes, flat-saucer domes, or polygonal domes—for example, the structurally ingenious double-shelled octagonal dome for the Renaissance Duomo in Florence by Filippo Brunelleschi, completed in 1436 and erected without scaffolding. Later, light and transparent cast-iron-and-glass domes for botanical gardens (for example, Kibble's Palace, Glasgow, of the 1860s) and arcades such as Giuseppe Mengoni's Galleria Vittorio Emanuele II, Milan 1877), were built. The 20th century saw the development of thin prestressed-reinforced-concrete shells and modular geodesic domes made of a web of thin steel struts filled with glass, plastic, fabrics, or ethylene tetrafluoroethylene (ETFE) pillows (for example, the Eden Project, Cornwall, UK, designed by Sir Nicholas Grimshaw).

3-SECOND FOUNDATION
A dome is a vaulted structure with a rotund shape and with a circular, polygonal, or elliptical base that allows for large clear-span structures.

3-MINUTE ELEVATION
A dome can be described as an arch revolved around its central axis. They are thus very stable and sound structures, since vertical arches and horizontal ring beams act together. Openings in domes are possible, as exemplified by the oculus, a round window at the apex of the dome. It is often crowned by a lantern, which gives additional stability to the structure through its own weight.

RELATED TOPICS
See also
THE ARCH
page 36

THE VAULT
page 40

3-SECOND BIOGRAPHIES
PIER LUIGI NERVI
1891–1979
Italian engineer, known for his large-span, prestressed reinforced-concrete structures

PAUL ANDREU
1938–
French architect, designer of the titanium-and-glass ellipsoid dome-shaped National Center for the Performing Arts, Beijing

30-SECOND TEXT
Marjan Colletti

Domes are a prominent feature in mosques and most Renaissance and Baroque cathedrals.

THE VAULT

the 30-second architecture

Simple vaults were used by the
Sumerians, Assyrians, Chaldeans, and Egyptians.
Later, Etruscans and Romans managed to erect
large vaulted amphitheaters, basilicas, and
thermae without buttresses. The largest ancient
vaults roofed the *iwan* hall of the Taq-i Kisra in
Ctesiphon, Iraq (141 ft), the Temple of Venus and
Roma (87 ft), the Basilica of Maxentius (82 ft),
and the throne hall in Diocletian's palace (98 ft)
in Rome. In the Middle Ages stonemasons
developed extremely complex and varied forms
of intersecting vaults. With the Gothic pointed
arch, vaults could be divided into four, six, or
more segments, with many arrises and ribs of
unequal width, yet intersecting at the same
height. Particular to England are fan vaults, the
most famous being King's College Chapel in
Cambridge (1536). Renaissance and Baroque
architecture abandoned the Gothic rib vault to
reinvent and further develop Roman vault types.
Up to the 20th century vaults were always
constructed in separate elements and enriched
with glass, frescoes, carvings, and sculptures.
In the 20th century, reinforced-concrete
technology, lightweight shell construction,
advanced structural engineering, and a better
understanding of geometric shapes such as
paraboloids facilitated the erection of impressive
slim-dimensioned shells, vaults, and domes.

3-SECOND FOUNDATION
A vault is an arched spatial
structure that spans a
void. Weight is carried
through the vault in
compression and into
supporting piers or
buttresses.

3-MINUTE ELEVATION
The most conventional
form is the semicircular or
pointed barrel (or wagon,
or tunnel) vault. Two
intersecting barrels of the
same diameter create a
groin (or cross) vault; the
resulting ridges are called
arrises. We speak of rib
vaults when barrel vaults
with matching or different
diameters transect, with
the groins subjected to
extra masonry work. A
particularly elaborate type
is the fan vault, with
equidistantly arrayed ribs
of the same curve.

RELATED TOPICS
See also
ROMAN
page 20

ROMANESQUE
page 24

GOTHIC
page 28

3-SECOND BIOGRAPHIES
JOSEPH PAXTON
1803–65
English architect, designer of
the Crystal Palace, London

LOUIS I. KAHN
1901–74
American architect, designer
of the vaulted Kimbell Art
Museum, Fort Worth, Texas

FÉLIX CANDELA OUTERIÑO
1910–97
Spanish architect, famous for
his extremely thin reinforced-
concrete shells

30-SECOND TEXT
Marjan Colletti

*Depending on height,
geometry, and curvature,
vaults can be load-bearing
structures or light canopies.*

THE BEAM

the 30-second architecture

3-SECOND FOUNDATION
There are many different types of beam, but in its simplest form a beam is a rigid horizontal load-bearing member supported at its ends.

3-MINUTE ELEVATION
The ability of a beam to withstand vertical forces may be judged intuitively by the span-to-depth ratio. This is defined by the relationship between the depth of a beam's cross section and the distance between the supports at either end. If the span is narrow and the section is thick, the beam may appear unnecessarily massive and unwieldy, whereas if the span is too wide and the section too thin, the beam may fail.

The beam is one of the oldest, most basic structural elements known to humans. Even before nomadic pastoralists started settling on the land and building permanent structures, the beam was used by people to construct temporary dwellings or to cross streams by means of a felled tree. Whether a small stick covering a makeshift shelter or a massive precast reinforced-concrete girder supporting the roof of a modern building, both are beams performing the same function of withstanding vertical loads across a void. These vertical forces are shared between the supports at either end of the beam and transferred through the structure. In architectural terms, these supports are usually the walls of the building or the columns in a timber, steel, or concrete frame. The beam also masquerades as other elements, such as joists, which span opposing walls to support the floors or ceilings of a building, or lintels that support the structure above windows or doors, or girders designed to span wide distances or carry particularly heavy loads. Traditionally, stone, wood, and metal were the most common materials used for beams, but in recent decades combinations of materials—notably reinforced, pretensioned, or posttensioned concrete—have greatly improved performance.

RELATED TOPICS
See also
THE ARCH
page 36

THE COLUMN
page 46

THE FRAME
page 50

MODERNISM
page 108

30-SECOND TEXT
Edward Denison

One of the most elemental structural components, the beam, in its simplest form, is a horizontal load-bearing member supported at each end.

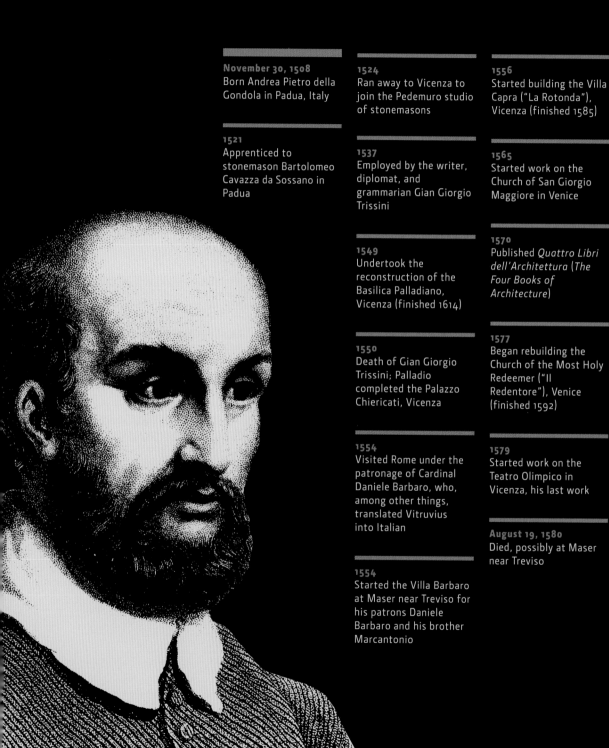

November 30, 1508
Born Andrea Pietro della Gondola in Padua, Italy

1521
Apprenticed to stonemason Bartolomeo Cavazza da Sossano in Padua

1524
Ran away to Vicenza to join the Pedemuro studio of stonemasons

1537
Employed by the writer, diplomat, and grammarian Gian Giorgio Trissini

1549
Undertook the reconstruction of the Basilica Palladiano, Vicenza (finished 1614)

1550
Death of Gian Giorgio Trissini; Palladio completed the Palazzo Chiericati, Vicenza

1554
Visited Rome under the patronage of Cardinal Daniele Barbaro, who, among other things, translated Vitruvius into Italian

1554
Started the Villa Barbaro at Maser near Treviso for his patrons Daniele Barbaro and his brother Marcantonio

1556
Started building the Villa Capra ("La Rotonda"), Vicenza (finished 1585)

1565
Started work on the Church of San Giorgio Maggiore in Venice

1570
Published *Quattro Libri dell'Architettura* (*The Four Books of Architecture*)

1577
Began rebuilding the Church of the Most Holy Redeemer ("Il Redentore"), Venice (finished 1592)

1579
Started work on the Teatro Olimpico in Vicenza, his last work

August 19, 1580
Died, possibly at Maser near Treviso

PALLADIO

Palladio—who showed 17th- and 18th-century Europe how to express the harmonies and proportions of Vitruvian Rome—is universally acknowledged as one of the seminal influences on Western architecture. He did not seem to be the most likely candidate for such fame to begin with. Born in 1508, Andrea Pietro della Gondola was a miller's son from Padua, apprenticed to a stern stonemason at the age of 13. He hated it, and when he was 16 he ran away to Padua where he joined another mason's yard. His big break came in 1537 when he was employed by humanist scholar Gian Giorgio Trissini to work on his villa at Chiericati. Trissini took to the young Gondola and introduced him to Renaissance culture, including the ideas of Vitruvius, and even gave him the name Palladio, meaning "the Wise One," after a character in one of his own poems, in turn named for the Greek goddess Pallas Athena. Palladio proved more than worthy of his patronage and began to make a name for himself from the 1540s onward. Industrious and gifted, he worked mostly around Venice and Vicenza, concentrating on church architecture, palaces, and, above all, villas, of which he produced around 30 that were inspired by the agricultural villas of ancient Rome. It is for the Villa Capra, also known as the "La Rotonda," that he is most famous. A harmonious, graceful, symmetrical edifice, built on Roman principles to a human scale, it influenced, among many others, Sir Christopher Wren, Inigo Jones—who paid homage to it in his Queen's House at Greenwich, London, of 1616—and Lord Burlington in England, and, in America, Thomas Jefferson, who based his design for Monticello, Virginia (1772), on it.

Palladio not only built prodigiously, he also published prolifically, producing a guide to the ruins of ancient Rome and contributing illustrations to Barbaro's edition of Vitruvius's *De Architectura*. His best-known work is *Quattro Libri dell'Architettura* (*The Four Books of Architecture*), in which he set out his principles of architecture, together with practical guidance for builders and a series of meticulous woodcuts. It became the standard text for architects in Europe, was translated into many European languages, and it remains in print today.

THE COLUMN

the 30-second architecture

The column (or pillar) is *the* fundamental structural unit of architecture. Using the column frees the wall so that, no longer acting as the load-bearing element, it can be treated purely as a covering. A column can be monolithic (of one single block of material, such as stone or wood), sectional (a single material, but sliced and stacked), or it can also be a combination of materials (concrete reinforced with steel). Typically, the column has three parts: capital (immediately supporting the beam, slab, or arch); shaft (the main body); and base (connecting the column to the foundation). Early civilizations such as Egypt and Babylonia decorated the column in all manner of shapes and forms. In Classical architecture, the column is codified in decorative orders, and the three parts of the column are treated differently according to which order is used. Classical architecture also uses carved female figures—caryatids—as columns. Columns can be half-set into a wall, forming pilasters. Columns soon became symbolic beyond their structural properties, placed in public spaces to commemorate persons or gods. Pilotis, or piers, are columns that support a whole building above ground; these have become a key feature of modern and contemporary architecture.

3-SECOND FOUNDATION
The column is a load-bearing structural element of architecture. It transmits the vertical forces of a beam, arch, or slab through compression to the foundation.

3-MINUTE ELEVATION
In his Domino House (1915) Le Corbusier argued that by using pilotis and columns instead of walls the architect had complete freedom in designing the plan and elevation. Another Modernist architect, Mies van der Rohe, is celebrated for his use of steel cruciform columns. Postmodern architects have played with the language of stability that the column suggests, cutting them in half or placing them at unusual angles.

RELATED TOPICS
See also
CLASSICAL GREEK
page 18

ROMAN
page 20

THE BEAM
page 42

CLASSICISM
page 98

3-SECOND BIOGRAPHIES
VITRUVIUS
fl. 46–30 BCE
Roman architect and theorist who recorded the earliest known codification of the orders of columns

LEON BATTISTA ALBERTI
1404–72
Italian architect and polymath who developed the theory that the column could be feminine or masculine in form

30-SECOND TEXT
Nick Beech

The column, as a fundamental structural unit in architecture, has become a symbol for "stability."

THE BUTTRESS

the 30-second architecture

The buttress solves a fundamental problem with the wall—at a certain height a wall can topple over under its own weight or from taking the load of a roof or arch. A buttress is any mass of material—such as stone, brick, or concrete—attached to the wall to prevent this. Buttresses are found in city walls and castles across the world—and particularly 11th-century Norman (Romanesque) church and castle architecture in Europe. They can be attached in a series along the face of a wall or at corners formed by the meeting of two walls. The buttress first appears as a continuous or stepped (wider at the base, thinner at the top) column. The flying buttress—detached from the wall and connected to it by an arch—was a key innovation that occurred at the end of the Romanesque and beginning of the Gothic periods. To add greater vertical thrust, the flying buttress is often capped with a heavy load above the arch called a pinnacle, and the history of Gothic architecture is, in part, the history of increasingly spectacular and daring uses of the flying buttress and decoration of the pinnacle.

3-SECOND FOUNDATION
The buttress is a structural element of a wall that resists lateral forces generated by the wall or from load-bearing of a roof or arch.

3-MINUTE ELEVATION
Buttresses are part of the history of the separation of two key qualities of the wall: the wall as a support (holding something up) and as a screen (making a space private). Gothic architecture is completely dependent on the use of the flying buttress as a support to replace a stone screen with a glass screen. In modern architecture, with the use of concrete and steel frames, the buttress is effectively redundant.

RELATED TOPICS
See also
ROMANESQUE
page 24

GOTHIC
page 28

THE ARCH
page 36

THE COLUMN
page 46

3-SECOND BIOGRAPHIES
EUGÈNE VIOLLET-LE-DUC
1814–79
French architect and theorist, who argued that innovations to the buttress in the 13th century radically transformed architecture

30-SECOND TEXT
Nick Beech

The buttress owes its aesthetic appeal to the fact that it expresses the structural forces of architecture.

THE FRAME

the 30-second architecture

3-SECOND FOUNDATION
A frame is a three-dimensional, lightweight system of connected struts. It provides the structural skeleton to a building and is essential for high-rise buildings.

3-MINUTE ELEVATION
Wood framing is still a common method of construction for apartment buildings in Canada and the United States, including balloon framing and the more recently developed platform framing. The former connects long timber studs and fabricates the walls first, with the floors subsequently attached to them. The latter joins smaller timber sticks to platforms, with the walls built on top of them. Diagonal bracing and paneling add rigidity and stability.

Compared with solid masonry constructions, frames are open, more efficient load-bearing structures made of columns, beams, trusses, girders, and spandrels. Many traditional construction techniques used wooden frames before the advent of iron and steel. The world's oldest iron-framed building is Ditherington Flax Mill, Shrewsbury, UK (Charles Bage, 1797), but high-rise steel frames really took off in Chicago, New York, and London because of the high land values. The world's first skyscraper was the 10-story Home Insurance Company Building in Chicago (William Le Baron Jenney, 1885), with a frame of cast-iron columns and wrought-iron beams. In the 20th century, reinforced concrete emerged as the main alternative to frame structures, either poured in situ or assembled from prefabricated elements. A frame does not need to be orthogonal. On the contrary, frames built up by a three-dimensional matrix of triangular and tetrahedral shapes are much more rigid and are often used for massive structures including hangars and bridges. Particularly unusual steel frames feature in the Olympic National Stadium in Beijing (Herzog & de Meuron, Arup and China Architecture Design & Research Group, 2008) and the BMW World Building in Munich (Coop Himmelb(l)au, 2007).

RELATED TOPICS
See also
THE DOME
page 38

LESS IS MORE
page 82

AVANT-GARDE
page 106

3-SECOND BIOGRAPHIES
WILLIAM LE BARON JENNEY
1832–1907
American architect, engineer, and pioneer of skyscrapers

LUDWIG MIES VAN DER ROHE
1886–1969
German–American architect who achieved free-flowing open spaces thanks to "skin-and-bone" frames

RICHARD ROGERS & RENZO PIANO
1933– & 1937–
British and Italian architects, co-creators of the Pompidou Center, Paris

30-SECOND TEXT
Marjan Colletti

A building's elements—concrete, timber, or steel—are usually assembled into a 3D frame.

PROJECTION

cutaway drawing A method of creating a three-dimensional effect and showing the inside of a building by selectively removing parts of the outer skin, while maintaining the overall shape and structure of the building.

exploded-view drawing Where the elements of a building are "exploded" to reveal their relationship with one another and how they fit and work together. Like the cutaway drawing, this was a Renaissance invention.

Fibonacci numbers Named after Italian mathematician Leonardo of Pisa, known as Fibonacci (c. 1170–c. 1250)—who introduced the concept into Western mathematics (although it had been known earlier to Indian mathematicians)—these are numbers that form a mathematical sequence, in which the following number is the sum of the previous two, so 0, 1, 1, 2, 3, 5, 8, 13. In art and architecture, the Fibonacci sequence is related to the perceived properties of the golden ratio.

golden ratio Also called the golden section or golden mean, this is a proportion believed to have some intrinsic aesthetic value that is in harmony with the universe. In practice, it has been defined as the effect created when a line is unequally divided, such that the whole is to the longer of the sections as that section is to the shorter.

human scale One of the scales in architecture in which a building is designed to work on a scale that makes humans feel in harmony with that environment. Other scales—monumental, for example—are created deliberately to work against it in order to create a specific psychological effect on those interacting with it.

Modulor system A system of measurement and proportion devised by Le Corbusier in the tradition of the writings of Vitruvius and da Vinci's "Vitruvian Man." It was based on the measurements of a 6-ft tall man and was designed to help work out the ideal proportions for living and working spaces on a human scale.

orthographic drawing A means of representing a three-dimensional object in two dimensions. In architectural practice, this is a blanket term used to cover three types of drawing: section (a vertical slice through a building); plan (a horizontal slice); and elevation (a depiction of a façade).

Palladianism A style of Renaissance architecture derived from the buildings and written works of Andrea Palladio (1508–80). Particularly notable for symmetrical designs and use of Classical harmony, an early practitioner was the 17th-century English architect Inigo Jones, and Palladian principles and elements later became an essential part of the vocabulary of Neoclassical architecture across Europe.

Raumplan Adolf Loos's (1870–1933) "space plan," in which he put the design emphasis on individual rooms according to purpose, rather than for rooms to be squeezed into predetermined and restrictive floors. As he said, "My architecture is not conceived in plans but in spaces ... For me there is no ground floor, first floor ... Stories merge and spaces relate to each other."

vanishing point A key concept in the system of perspective—first appearing in the early 15th century—in which it is understood that while parallel lines can never meet in reality, in art they will appear to do so. So all parallel lines in a painting going in one direction will ultimately meet at a single point, the vanishing point, in order to create the illusion of three-dimensional space.

"Vitruvian Man" A drawing (c. 1487) by Leonardo da Vinci, derived from the writings of Vitruvius to depict the ideal proportions for geometry based on the human body.

THE PLAN

the 30-second architecture

A floor plan in architecture looks very similar to a map—it is a scaled drawing that includes all the fixed features of a defined area as if you were looking at it from above. However, for a drawing to be a plan it must have at least two other qualities. First, it is like a horizontal section—it "cuts" along a horizontal plane (typically about 4 ft above the ground), showing the thickness of walls (with a hatched or black infill) and the interior space of a building (clear or textured to indicate a floor surface). Second, it includes outlines of features that are below that cut—fixed or permanent furniture, for example. For any single building, a number of plans need to be drawn to show the ground level, first floor, second floor, and so on, all of which can be quite different. A plan is usually monotone (often black on white) and is always measured and to scale. The plan has always been, and remains, one of the fundamental projections, or drawings, by which architects are able to develop a scheme because it demonstrates the arrangement and sequence of spaces.

RELATED TOPICS
See also
SECTION
page 58

SCALE
page 68

3-SECOND BIOGRAPHIES
HANNES MEYER
1889–1954
Swiss architect, head of the Bauhaus school (1927–30)

JACQUES-FRANÇOIS BLONDEL
1705–74
Highly influential French architect and theorist

ROBIN EVANS
1944–93
British architect and historian who wrote on the cultural and social significance of drawing architecture

30-SECOND TEXT
Nick Beech

3-SECOND FOUNDATION
Plans are the fundamental drawings used to organize space, which, drawn to scale, provide information on solid elements (walls, stairs, doors) and the spaces between.

3-MINUTE ELEVATION
Le Corbusier famously proclaimed that "the plan is the generator." This plays on two meanings, "a plan" being a kind of drawing, and "to plan," meaning to consciously organize future action. By drawing a plan, space and the people who use it are organized in a particular way. This idea is not new, as we can see Classical, Gothic, Renaissance, and 18th-century architects approaching the plan in a similar way.

An ability to read a plan is a key skill in architecture, since the plan represents how a building is organized.

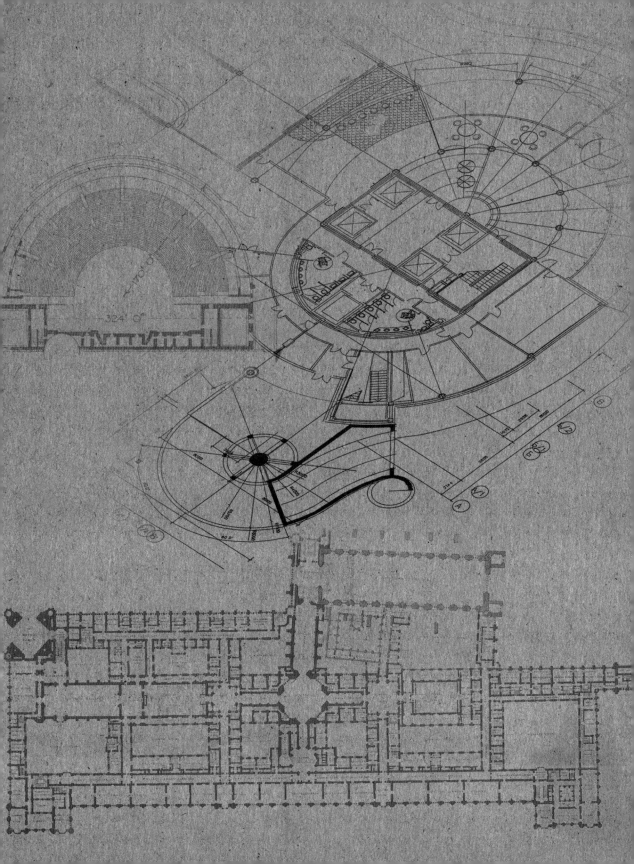

SECTION

the 30-second architecture

A section slices through a building to produce a two-dimensional representation of a building's profile, as well as an elevation of its interior. Sections are generally understood to be vertical cuts through a building, although a plan is, in effect, simply a horizontal section. Sometimes difficult to read for the untrained eye, a section serves as a medium of communication between architects, consultants, and other professionals to define the exact vertical measurements of a structure. The section as a dominant form of architectural representation emerged in the 16th century from the archaeological contemplation and sketching of the ruins of ancient structures. It was the barren and cracked walls and vaults of buildings—such as the Baths of Caracalla or the Colosseum in Rome—that gave rise to the idea of "slicing" open a building to reveal its internal workings through the medium of drawing. In a 1527 treatise on military architecture, Albrecht Dürer was the first to present a section aligned with a plan and an elevation, thus promoting the idea of these three orthographic types of drawings belonging together as a set.

3-SECOND FOUNDATION
The section is a drawing produced from an imaginary, usually vertical, cut through a structure, revealing its outline and the interior visible behind the cut.

3-MINUTE ELEVATION
The Modernist architect Adolf Loos prioritized the section over the plan when designing a building. With his *Raumplan* (space plan) theory, he intended to liberate the building from its fixed vertical divisions into floors, assigning different heights for each room according to its use and social importance within the building. Loos claimed to design by adding cubes on top and next to each other, rather than working with flat floor plans.

RELATED TOPICS
See also
THE PLAN
page 56

ELEVATION
page 60

SCALE
page 68

CAD
page 142

3-SECOND BIOGRAPHIES
ALBRECHT DÜRER
1471–1528
German printmaker, painter, draftsman, and writer. A key driver of the Renaissance in Northern Europe

ADOLF LOOS
1870–1933
Austrian Modernist architect and writer, who promoted a focus on function and economy in architectural design

30-SECOND TEXT
Anne Hultzsch

A section view of a building reveals its load-bearing structure as well as an internal elevation.

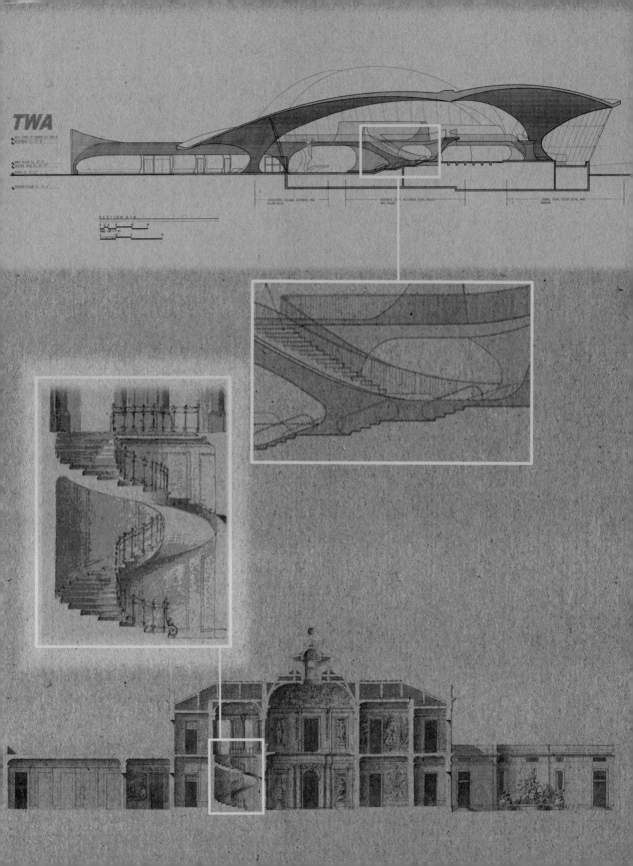

TWA

ELEVATION

the 30-second architecture

RELATED TOPICS
See also
THE PLAN
page 56

SECTION
page 58

PERSPECTIVE
page 64

SCALE
page 68

3-SECOND BIOGRAPHIES
JOHN HEJDUK
1929–2000
American architect/artist with
an interest in the creative and
theoretical possibilities of
architectural drawing

ROBIN EVANS
1944–93
British architect, teacher, and
historian, known for pioneering
work on architectural drawings

30-SECOND TEXT
Anne Hultzsch

3-SECOND FOUNDATION
As a drawing, an elevation
depicts the front of a
building in an orthogonal
projection, showing
accurate dimensions
of all its parts.

3-MINUTE ELEVATION
In *The Projective Cast*
(1995), architect and
historian Robin Evans
suggested that the reliance
on orthographic drawing,
including the elevation,
has promoted the
prevalence of rectangular
shapes in buildings. As the
projective plane employed
to construct an elevation is
flat and straight and not
curved, it encourages the
design of flat and straight
elevations in buildings.
With the rise of computer-
aided design and
three-dimensional
modeling, in recent
decades architectural
design has produced more
non-orthogonal schemes.

Generally speaking, an elevation
denotes a particular side of a building, or one of
its façades, which can be front, back, or any of
the sides. More specifically, it describes the type
of drawing made from projecting a building's
façade at right angles onto a vertical plane
parallel to that façade (or an imaginary flat
surface, if the façade is curved). Along with an
accompanying plan and section, the elevation is
consistently scaled, and thus forms part of the
orthographic set of drawings used to define a
structure's exact measurements. Vitruvius wrote
in *De Architectura* (c. 15 BCE) that an "elevation
is a picture of the front of a building, set upright
and properly drawn in the proportions of the
contemplated work." From the Renaissance
onward, but especially in 18th- and early
19th-century drawings, elevations were often
combined with perspective to show more
depth and reveal recesses and projections,
also emphasized by using shading. More
recently, in the 20th century, axonometric
projections have taken over a similar role, while
today computer-generated three-dimensional
models allow for unlimited numbers of
orthographic projections in any plane.

*An elevation presents
accurate measurements
of a building's façade,
as well as an easily
recognizable image.*

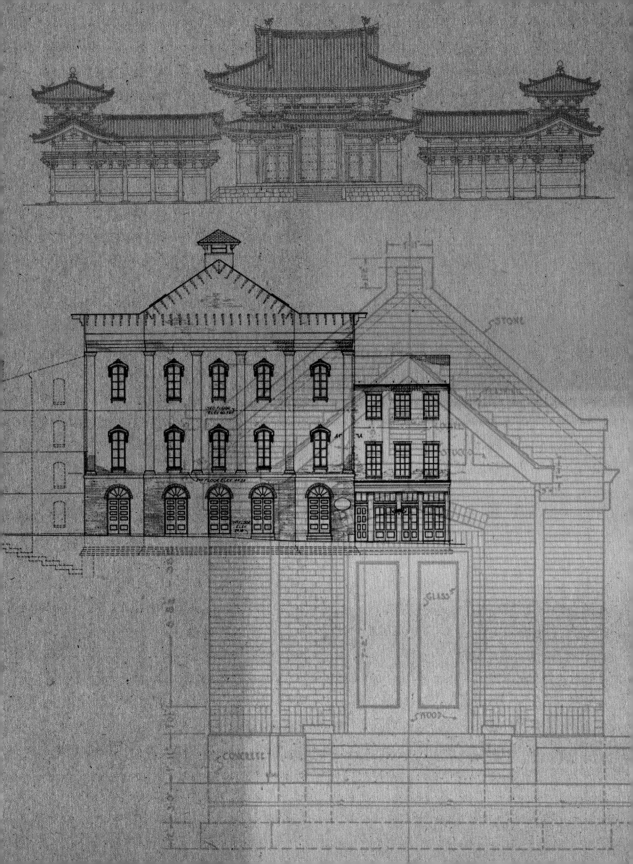

SYMMETRY

the 30-second architecture

Symmetry is perhaps the most easily accessible idea within the wider realm of architectural geometry and number systems. The principle is a familiar one, that one side of an image is a close match of the other. Egyptian pyramids can be described as embodying this principle, as can other examples from antiquity such as the Parthenon in Athens or Rome's Pantheon. Classical buildings will almost always feature an equal number of columns along a façade so that the entrance can be placed centrally—an unequal number of columns or compositional devices would force the entrance to be placed off-center. The 16th-century Italian architect Palladio took ideas of symmetry to an extreme, notably in his Villa Capra (1560): each of its four façades is identical, and the plan of the building (a small circle within a larger square) is entirely symmetrical either side of both axes. Neoclassical architects after the Renaissance employed symmetry as part of their design language, including Lord Burlington in Britain (Holkham Hall and Chiswick House) and the USA's John Russell Pope (Jefferson Memorial). The Capitol building in Washington, DC, built and extended throughout the 19th century, is a prime example of the power of symmetry.

3-SECOND FOUNDATION
Symmetry is the principle that a building, in plan or elevation, is broadly mirrored either side of a central axis.

3-MINUTE ELEVATION
As a rule of thumb, Classical architecture tends to embody the principle of symmetry, whereas Gothic and medieval architecture is more variable. The (largely) 19th-century Palace of Westminster in London, a Gothic design, is distinctly asymmetrical in form, in spite of the strict compositional rhythms of its surface. The works of some architects today—notably Frank Gehry and Daniel Libeskind—are celebrations of asymmetry.

RELATED TOPICS
See also
CLASSICAL GREEK
page 18

ROMAN
page 20

3-SECOND BIOGRAPHIES
LORD BURLINGTON
1694–1753
English nobleman, architect, and promoter of Palladianism

INIGO JONES
1573–1652
English architect responsible for bringing Italian Classical style to England

FRANK GEHRY
1929–
Canadian-American architect, designer of the Guggenheim in Bilbao, Spain, and the Walt Disney Concert Hall, Los Angeles

30-SECOND TEXT
David Littlefield

Symmetry, often symbolic of geometric purity, can manifest itself in elevation and in plan.

PERSPECTIVE

the 30-second architecture

Background for the development

of perspective as a graphical-representation technique dates from the art of the late medieval period. As art began to adopt more representational techniques, Renaissance artists such as Leonardo da Vinci and Albrecht Dürer studied the methods required for constructing realistic perspective images. In the 17th century, Blaise Pascal and Gérard Desargues were among the first mathematicians to explore perspective in a way that would establish it as a vital tool in architecture, art, and engineering. With the development of the theory of projective geometry in the 19th century through the work of Jean-Victor Poncelet, Karl von Staudt, August Ferdinand Möbius, and Jakob Steiner, perspective became a formal mathematical inquiry. In these studies the most important elements are the distance of objects from the eye of the observer and the illusion of depth within the constructed space, which is created through one or more vanishing points. Today, with advances in computer-generated three-dimensional modeling, a perspective image is easily constructed with the use of appropriate software. These can be rendered in any number of ways according to the purpose, as photorealistic or any other suitable style.

3-SECOND FOUNDATION
Perspective is a two-dimensional representation of three-dimensional space that architects use to depict the environments they create.

3-MINUTE ELEVATION
Early theories of how the eye perceives the world were explored by the Greek mathematician Euclid, who stated that the eye projects visual rays onto an object and the resulting perception of the world occurs as a dynamic activity of the observer. Alhazen, a Muslim scientist, made significant contributions to the principles of optics in the early 11th century, one of which was the idea that we see because rays of light enter the eye.

RELATED TOPICS
See also
SCALE
page 68

3-SECOND BIOGRAPHIES
EUCLID
fl. 300 BCE
Greek mathematician, the "father of geometry," author of *Optics*, the earliest surviving Greek work on perspective

LEONARDO DA VINCI
1452–1519
Italian Renaissance polymath, who experimented with perspective in his paintings

ALBRECHT DÜRER
1471–1528
German painter, engraver, mathematician, and theorist of perspective

30-SECOND TEXT
Dragana Cebzan Antic

Perspective is used to depict the space inside and outside of the building that usually shows an image as it would be seen from the eye level view.

AXONOMETRIC PROJECTION

the 30-second architecture

Axonometric drawings are a relatively recent technique (c. 19th century), first developed as tools for the analysis of structures. They look like strange, distorted perspective drawings—paradoxically, because axonometric drawings are mathematically precise. In perspective, parallel lines converge, while in axonometric, parallel lines remain parallel—they never meet. This is because in axonometric projection all measures at all three planes—height, width, depth—remain constant. Therefore, all component parts of a structure and the spaces between are given a precise, measurable relationship. This makes it very powerful for the architect. An axonometric image can either be given as a bird's-eye view, looking down onto the corner of a building, or a worm's-eye view, looking up into the corner of a building. Various techniques are used to show parts of a building that would otherwise be hidden by walls, ceilings, or roofs, including: cutaways, as if parts of the building have been peeled off; wire frame, showing all the edges where surfaces meet, as if the building were made of wire; and exploded, as if the building were an assemblage of parts that had been extruded along horizontal and vertical planes.

RELATED TOPICS
See also
PERSPECTIVE
page 64

THE PLAN
page 56

SECTION
page 58

SCALE
page 68

3-SECOND FOUNDATION
Axonometric projection in its various forms—isometric, diametric, trimetric, and oblique—is a powerful tool for analyzing and constructing three-dimensional space on a two-dimensional surface.

3-MINUTE ELEVATION
Axonometric drawing was first formalized in the 19th century as "isometry" ("equal measure") by the natural philosopher William Farish. French Rationalist architects of the period found it useful in analyzing ancient structures, and it became a key form of projection for Modernists, suiting their view of architecture as rational and machinelike. Common in Europe until the Renaissance development of perspectival projection, axonometric drawing continued to be used elsewhere, notably in China.

3-SECOND BIOGRAPHIES
AUGUSTE CHOISY
1841–1909
French Rationalist architect

THEO VAN DOESBURG
1883–1931
Dutch artist, architect, and founder of De Stijl, who used axonometric projection to powerful visual effect

30-SECOND TEXT
Nick Beech

James Stirling (1926–92) made axonometric projection an art form: here, the History Faculty Library at Cambridge University.

SCALE

the 30-second architecture

In architectural practice, scale refers most commonly to the relationship that exists between a building and its representation in terms of size and complexity. It is used in plan or model scales, say 1:100, which means that one part in the plan or model is equal to 100 parts of the real thing. Scale also describes the idea of proportionality, as when we speak of a building being "out of scale." This points to a break in continuity of a common set of size relationships preeminent in a place—for instance, if a large-scale 10-story office complex occupying a whole block is inserted into a residential neighborhood of smaller-scale four-story buildings, it will create an imbalance in the relative scale. Finally, there is the concept of human scale, which pertains to the idea that an environment can either promote or inhibit human comfort and interaction. Leonardo da Vinci's so-called "Vitruvian Man" (c. 1490) as well as Le Corbusier's "Modulor" (1948)—a scale of proportions based on the human form, the Fibonacci numbers, and the golden ratio—were both attempts to link human proportions to an ideal scale in buildings.

RELATED TOPICS
See also
THE PLAN
page 56

SECTION
page 58

ELEVATION
page 60

PROPORTION &
THE GOLDEN RATIO
page 76

3-SECOND FOUNDATION
Scale describes the size relationship between a whole and its parts, or between an object and its representation.

3-MINUTE ELEVATION
The meaning of scale is today challenged by seemingly scale-less computer-aided design, in which we zoom into and out of drawings with a scroll of a mouse. While in paper drawings scale is determined by the draftsperson, virtual CAD models enable the viewer to smoothly switch scales in real time. As this is not automatically accompanied by an increase or reduction of detail shown, scale is in danger of becoming peripheral to architectural production.

3-SECOND BIOGRAPHIES
LEONARDO DA VINCI
1452–1519
Italian painter and polymath with strong interests in architectural theory and design

LE CORBUSIER
1887–1965
Swiss-French architect, designer, and urbanist, a pioneer of modern architecture

30-SECOND TEXT
Anne Hultzsch

Mathematical ratios, buildings, and their components, even the human form, depend on the concept of scale.

October 6, 1887
Born in La Chaux-de-Fonds, Switzerland

1907
Worked in Paris for architect Auguste Perret

1908
Studied architecture in Vienna with Josef Hoffman

1910–11
Worked in Berlin with architect Peter Behrens

1911
Traveled to the Balkans and Greece; made drawings of Classical Greek architecture

1914–15
Worked on a theoretical project known as the Domino House

1918
Returned to Paris and took up painting after meeting Cubist Amédée Ozenfant; published their manifesto on Purism and the journal *L'Ésprit Nouveau* (1920–5)

1922
Worked on Immeubles Villas, tower blocks of social housing, and designed private houses

1922
Put forward his unrealized scheme for the *Ville Contemporaine*

1923
Published *Vers une Architecture*

1925
Devised the Plan Voisin, an unrealized urban-renewal scheme for Paris

1925
Published *L'Art Décoratif d'Aujourd'hui* which railed against craft traditions and ornamentation

1927
Designed Villa Stein

1929–31
Designed Villa Savoye, an exemplar of his Five Points theory as defined in *Vers une Architecture*

1935
Published *La Ville Radieuse*, redefining his theories of urbanism

1946–52
Designed Unités d'Habitation—residential housing projects

1948
Published *Le Modulor*, an anthropometric scale of proportions

1950–4
Designed chapel of Notre Dame du Haut, Ronchamp

1952–9
Developed Chandigarh, India's first planned city

1953
Designed monastery of Ste-Marie de la Tourette, Éveux

August 25, 1965
Died at Roquebrune-Cap-Martin, France

Celebrated and derided, vilified

and deified, Le Corbusier polarized opinion among fellow architects and the general public, and his work is still reassessed and re-evaluated today. Born Charles-Édouard Jeanneret-Gris in Switzerland, in 1920 he reinvented himself as Le Corbusier, his name becoming almost a brand for his activities as an artist, theorist, writer, furniture designer, architect, and town planner.

Early experience in the offices of Auguste Perret (the pioneer of reinforced concrete) and Peter Behrens (where he would have come across Walter Gropius and Mies van der Rohe) had a great influence on him. After a period as an artist, in 1922 he set up a practice in Paris with his cousin Pierre Jeanneret and worked mostly on private villas, notably the Villa Savoye at Poissy, which embodied his Five Points of Architecture. Using steel, glass, reinforced concrete, and the aesthetic of an ocean liner, this is now regarded as the quintessential Corbusier construction.

In 1923 he published the influential *Vers une Architecture* [*Toward an Architecture*], which outlined his concept of a planned city that would eliminate the slums and squalor that could lead to social unrest. Le Corbusier went on to work on various ambitious urban-planning projects, publishing his ideas in *La Ville Radieuse* (*The Radiant City*)—which was influenced by the garden-city movement—which culminated in his work on Chandigarh, the new capital of the Punjab in India, for which he devised the plan and many of the buildings.

He also developed his Modulor system as a guide to proportion in domestic building based on human proportions. He applied this to the Unités d'Habitation tower blocks—his *machines à vivre*—which were built in various French cities, the one in Marseilles being the best known. On the back of these, Le Corbusier has been blamed for the blight of grim, alienating tower bocks all over northern Europe—although his supporters argue that his ideas have been misunderstood and misappropriated. However, he was without question also capable of reaching the sublime, which he did most effectively in the chapel of Notre Dame du Haut at Ronchamp. A departure from Corbusian standardization, it is at once simple and complex, using plain materials with an upturning heaven-seeking roof, yet the space within is made mysterious and transcendent, full of veiled light from a series of asymmetric windows punctuating the thick, unadorned walls.

THEORIES/CONCEPTS

THEORIES/CONCEPTS
GLOSSARY

"as found" An artistic approach that found its expression in architecture in the 1950s with the Independent Group and the New Brutalists. In essence, "as found" is concerned with finding authenticity in the everyday, the raw, and advocated architecture that displayed its materials and structure without superfluous decorative embellishment.

Constructivism More than a movement or style in art and architecture, Constructivism was a whole aesthetic. Finding its widest expression in the early years of the USSR, in the 1920s and early 1930s it was the dominant style for Soviet public architecture, displaying a utilitarian simplicity and respect for materials. After the rise in a kind of Renaissance pastiche architecture under Stalin, Constructivism lived on in the West through the Bauhaus and its legacy.

figure–ground diagrams A type of drawing that depicts the relationship between foreground and background through contrasting colors. This is used in urban design to show how built-up space (often in black) works with the void around it (white).

Functionalism The principle that, above all else, a building should function well for its intended purpose and any design aesthetic should not interfere with that.

Gestalt psychology The idea that the whole is greater than the sum of its constituent parts and that the human mind perceives the whole object before breaking it down into individual elements. The best-known example of this is the faces–vase drawing, where, depending on your perception, you either see two faces in profile, facing one another, or a vase. This principle is behind the solid–void theory in architecture and figure–ground drawings.

Minimalism An approach to design that dispenses with unnecessary and frivolous elements, which first arose in the 19th century as a reaction to the overdecorated styles of the 18th century but continued right through the 20th. In architecture it is expressed in clean lines and a reduction of all elements to their simplest, leanest forms—"less is more," as Mies van der Rohe said.

picturesque An artistic concept, which became very much part of Romantic thinking in the 19th century, where a landscape or building looks as if it could either have come from or be the subject of a painting. In architecture it is characterized by asymmetrical forms and textural variety. Related to the concept of the sublime and beautiful.

Postmodern Historicism Where elements from previous styles are used on a contemporary building. One notable example is the decorative "Chippendale" pediment on Philip Johnson and John Burgee's essentially Modernist Sony Tower (formerly the AT&T Building, 1984).

Prairie School A school of architecture of the late 19th and early 20th centuries that sought to find an indigenous American style of architecture, unrelated to European forms although influenced by Arts & Crafts. Centered on the US Midwest, and most famously found in the work of Frank Lloyd Wright, a horizontal emphasis and integration with the surrounding landscape are two of its characteristics.

Revivalism Term covering any revival of an earlier form of architecture, such as 18th-century Neoclassicism or the Tudor Revival of the early 20th century.

sublime and beautiful In the 18th century the British philosopher Edmund Burke argued that the two were mutually exclusive: beauty requires light, while the sublime requires intense light or darkness for its effect.

truth to materials A principle of Modernist architecture, in which the materials of a building's construction are not hidden or disguised.

utilitas, venustas, firmitas According to Vitruvius in *De Architectura*, the three qualities—the Vitruvian Triad—that any structure must have: solidity, usefulness, beauty.

Utopian Idealist—often impractical—ideas.

PROPORTION & THE GOLDEN RATIO

the 30-second architecture

3-SECOND FOUNDATION
Proportion refers to the measurable relation (or ratio) of parts (a column, step, or beam, for example) to the whole of any given building.

3-MINUTE ELEVATION
Le Corbusier developed a system of proportions that integrated the golden ratio, "Vitruvian Man," the metric meter, and the British imperial foot. Called the Modulor, Le Corbusier elaborated the system in two books and designed a tape measure. The idea was that whole towns could be designed using the Modulor system. Based on a 6-ft-tall man, the system was—thankfully for those shorter or taller— never fully realized.

For Vitruvius, architecture was the "balanced adjustment of the details to the whole, the arrangement of proportion with a view to a symmetrical result." By this he meant that every different part of a building should measurably relate to every other part so as to achieve harmony. The ancient Greeks and earlier civilizations had identified such relationships of distinct parts to wholes in nature. The human body—the hand, the foot, the forearm (cubit)— provided a set of related measures (or units) that could be used to decide the length, height, and breadth of any given object or space. Renaissance architects turned Vitruvius's system of proportions into a complete humanist philosophy. The result was "Vitruvian Man," which systematically mapped onto the human body ratios found in mathematics, music, and Classical architecture. From Leon Battista Alberti in the 15th century onward, the idea that architectural proportions should be based on the human body was merged with abstract ratios discovered in geometry, particularly the golden ratio. The golden ratio was first defined by Euclid in c. 300 BCE: if a line is cut into two parts, the whole should be to the greater part as the greater part is to the shorter.

RELATED TOPICS
See also
CLASSICAL GREEK
page 18

ROMAN
page 20

SCALE
page 68

3-SECOND BIOGRAPHIES
ARISTOTLE
c. 384–22 BCE
Greek philosopher who put proportionality at the center of his aesthetics and ethics

LEON BATTISTA ALBERTI
1404–72
Italian architect and author of *De Re Aedificatoria* (*On the Art of Building*)

COLIN ROWE
1920–99
British-American art historian, architectural critic, and author

30-SECOND TEXT
Nick Beech

Once elaborated, the golden ratio can be traced onto all manner of architecture.

FORM FOLLOWS FUNCTION

the 30-second architecture

RELATED TOPICS
See also
AVANT-GARDE
page 106

MODERNISM
page 108

INTERNATIONAL STYLE
page 130

3-SECOND FOUNDATION
"Form follows function"
is a tenet of 20th-century
architecture, which
suggests that a building's
intended function should
be the principal factor in
its design.

3-MINUTE ELEVATION
The root of functional
architecture can be found
in the work of Roman
theorist Vitruvius, who
claimed that architectural
structure must exhibit
three qualities: *utilitas*,
venustas, and *firmitas*
(utility, attractiveness,
stability). *Utilitas* concerns
ease of use; *venustas*
involves aesthetics and
the architect's artistic
expression; and *firmitas*
refers to strength of
construction not only in
terms of carrying its own
weight, but also its ability
to withstand the elements.

"Form follows function" was
coined by American architect Louis Sullivan to
express the trend among European and
American architects to sideline and even reject
decoration. The most extreme expression of this
thinking was found in the work of Adolf Loos,
who said that "ornament is a crime," as he
believed that the omission of ornamentation
from everyday objects would aid cultural
advancement. The two principles were adopted
by Modernist architects in their promotion of
industrial aesthetics and simple, undecorated
artifacts, and this approach influenced the
development of new building types—notably
the first skyscrapers. Although the rapid rise
in the popularity of skyscrapers was propelled
largely by commercial concerns, Sullivan hoped
that the purely profit-driven nature of such
developments could be transcended by excellent
design and subtle ornamentation. Over time,
these ideas informed what became known as
Functionalism, whereby an architect's aesthetic
and artistic concerns should never interfere with
a building's function. Skyscraper developments
rapidly advanced the technology of materials
used—such as steel, concrete, and glass—which
gave rise to the relatively plain curtain-wall
façade that dominated much of mid-20th-
century public and commercial architecture.

3-SECOND BIOGRAPHIES
LOUIS SULLIVAN
1856–1924
American architect, known as
the father of the skyscraper

FRANK LLOYD WRIGHT
1867–1959
American architect, interior
designer, and educator, a
leader of the Prairie School
movement

ADOLF LOOS
1870–1933
Austro-Hungarian architect,
known for his critique of
decoration and ornamentation
in architecture

30-SECOND TEXT
Dragana Cebzan Antic

*Despite his Modernist
views, Louis Sullivan
used Art Nouveau floral
motifs in his Auditorium.*

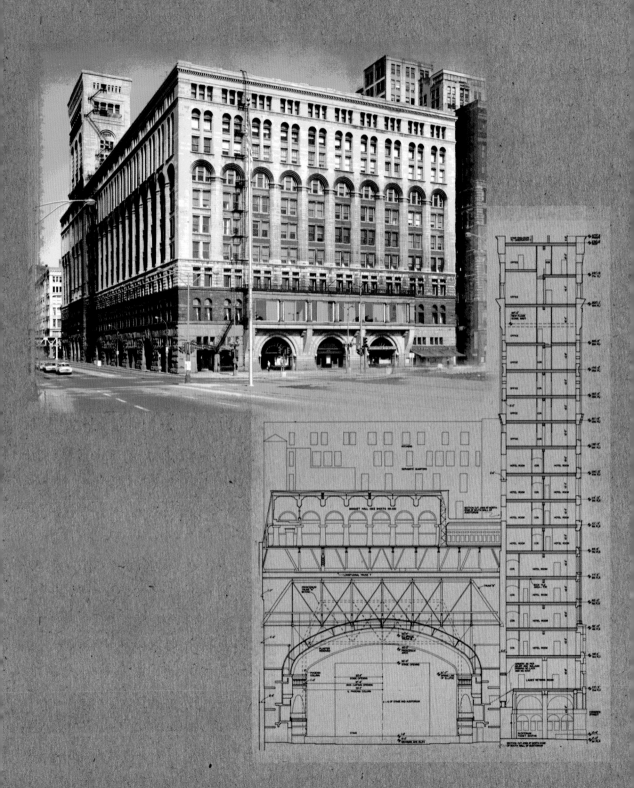

SOLID–VOID

the 30-second architecture

Solid–void theory works on the concept that what the architect designs is as much the (solid) mass of a building as the (void) spaces surrounding and enveloping it. It is based on the concept of positive (built) versus negative (open) space, so, in this sense, the façades of buildings lining a street become the walls shaping the volume of space making up that street. Solid–void theory thus encourages the architect and planner to give equal, if not more, importance to the design of open space than to that of built space. In urban design this becomes particularly relevant through the use of figure–ground diagrams, essentially maps or plans marking all built space in solid black (figure), while all open space remains white (ground). Frederick Gibberd, designer of the new town of Harlow, UK (1947–72), promoted the reversal of such diagrams, presenting buildings in white and open space in black in an attempt to put emphasis on the design of space itself rather than built matter. In *Collage City* (1978), architectural critic Colin Rowe analyzed several large cities through figure–ground plans, arguing that each city had been produced through a continuous process of superimposition and collage of objects, structures, and textures.

RELATED TOPICS
See also
THE PLAN
page 56

3-SECOND FOUNDATION
In architecture, solid–void theory describes the relationship between built and open space, while regarding both as contained volumes equally important to the designer.

3-MINUTE ELEVATION
Solid–void and figure–ground theories are derived from Gestalt psychology and best known from optical illusions such as the famous faces–vase drawing by Edgar Rubin. Depending on which part of the image, white or black, is perceived as containing volume, the viewer will identify in Rubin's illustration either a vase or two faces. The Dutch artist M. C. Escher exploited this phenomenon in his impossible architectural figures, which constitute veritable visual puzzles.

3-SECOND BIOGRAPHIES
M. C. ESCHER
1898–1972
Dutch printmaker, known for art often showing ambiguous or impossible perspectives

FREDERICK GIBBERD
1908–84
British architect and town planner

COLIN ROWE
1920–99
British-American architectural critic and teacher, who promoted an eclectic style and the use of collage in design

30-SECOND TEXT
Anne Hultzsch

White v. black, built v. open space: solid–void theory uses graphic effects to illustrate the interaction between a building and its surroundings.

LESS IS MORE

the 30-second architecture

The concept of "less is more" developed into a rational architectural approach that was reflected in the organization, planning, and detailing of buildings. The term encapsulates the concept of architectural necessity, in which redundant architectural elements are rendered superfluous, resulting in the flattening and emphasizing of a building's structural frame and the adoption of the open-plan space, which dispensed with interior walls. For this reason it is often compared with the rejection of ornamentation advocated by the architect Adolf Loos, but Mies van der Rohe's form of Minimalism was less extreme and allowed a degree of decoration if it did not detract from the overall design. Mies termed this "skin-and-bones" architecture, in which structure was reduced to a transparent, strong, and elegant skin. For advocates of this approach, order and meaning are achieved through basic geometrical forms, simple use of materials, undecorated elements, and the repetition of structure. The roots of this can be found in the Arts & Crafts movement, which promoted "truth to materials," meaning that materials should be used honestly to reflect their profound and innate natural characteristics with no artifice.

3-SECOND FOUNDATION
The term "less is more" was coined by the architect Mies van der Rohe and encapsulated his design philosophy, and that of the Minimalist movement.

3-MINUTE ELEVATION
By eliminating all non-essential forms or elements, "less is more" searches for the essential quality of a building's identity. The approach was criticized for being too abstract and not adequately addressing the user's emotional needs in the way that other styles did. On the other hand, the geometrical abstraction of Minimalism can be understood as essentially simplified scenery that does not impose itself on the environment, but becomes part of it.

RELATED TOPICS
See also
ARTS & CRAFTS
page 104

AVANT-GARDE
page 106

MODERNISM
page 108

3-SECOND BIOGRAPHIES
WALTER GROPIUS
1883–1969
German architect and founder of the Bauhaus School

LUDWIG MIES VAN DER ROHE
1886–1969
German-American architect and a pioneer of modern architecture

OSCAR NIEMEYER
1907–2012
Brazilian architect, one of the early Modernist architects

30-SECOND TEXT
Dragana Cebzan Antic

The concept is shown by flat façades with straight lines, a strong geometrical style, and no ornamentation.

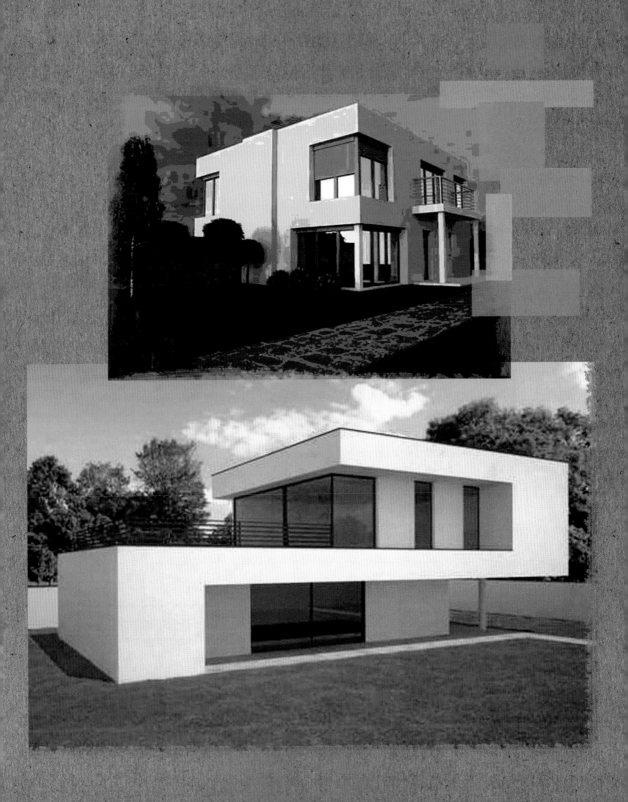

September 3, 1856
Born in Boston, Massachusetts

1872
Began studying at Massachusetts Institute of Technology

1873
Worked with architect Frank Furness

1873
Moved to Chicago and worked for architect William Le Baron Jenney

1874
Moved to Paris to study at the École des Beaux-Arts

1875
Back in Chicago working as draftsman in the office of architects Joseph S. Johnston and John Edelman

1879
Began working with Dankmar Adler, becoming his partner

1886–90
Adler and Sullivan work on the Auditorium Building, Chicago

1891
Adler and Sullivan begin work on the Wainwright building in St. Louis, Missouri, one of the world's first skyscrapers

1892
Completed the Wainwright Tomb, St. Louis, Missouri

1893
Chicago World's Fair; Sullivan was one of the 10 architects chosen to make a contribution

1894
The Chicago Stock Exchange and the Prudential Building (aka the Guaranty Building), Buffalo, New York, finished

1894
Adler and Sullivan dissolved their partnership

1897–9
Worked on the Bayard-Condict Building in Manhattan, his only building in New York

1899–1904
Worked on the Carson, Pirie, and Scott Building, a Chicago department store

1908
Worked on the National Farmers' Bank in Owatonna, Minnesota

1912–14
Worked on the Van Allen Building, a department store in Clinton, Iowa

April 14, 1924
Died in Chicago

LOUIS SULLIVAN

Born in Boston, Louis Henry

Sullivan would become forever associated with the thrusting, muscular architecture of Chicago. Known now as one of the founding fathers both of the skyscraper and of Modernism, he coined the phrase branded onto the heart of every modern architect: "form follows function." What he actually said was, "form ever follows function," and although later architects, particularly the International School, took this to mean buildings should be stripped of all ornament, Sullivan himself gave ornamentation—particularly intricate Art Nouveau floral motifs—a function, making it the invaluable punctuation in the grammar of the new high-rise architecture.

After only a year of study at the Massachusetts Institute of Technology, Sullivan talked his way into various architectural firms, took a year off in Paris to study at the École des Beaux-Arts, and finally set up in partnership with the dynamic Dankmar Adler in Chicago. Specializing in theater buildings then offices, they had 256 projects and commissions, including the iconic Auditorium Building in Chicago, the Prudential (or Guaranty) Building in Buffalo, New York, and the Wainwright Building in St. Louis, Missouri.

Sullivan abhorred the heavy masonry of the Classical style and embraced the freedom granted by steel, understanding its potential and how to articulate the new slender shape of the high-rise building it made possible.

Difficult economic conditions in 1893 meant the end for the Adler and Sullivan partnership. Working alone, Sullivan finished one of his greatest works, the Carson, Pirie, and Scott Building, a department store in Chicago. Following this, while he continued to find commissions—this was the period of his "jewel boxes," nine exquisite buildings for banks in the Midwest, all still standing—life and work became harder for Sullivan, and he died in poverty in 1924.

As his style fell out of favor through the mid-20th century, many of his works were demolished, and it was not until the 1970s that efforts were made to preserve his extant buildings and collect as many remnants as could be found of those that had been demolished, including a whole floor of the Chicago Stock Exchange, splendidly reconstructed at the Art Institute of Chicago. Sullivan left an indelible architectural legacy and a distinctive and rigorous vocabulary for the architecture that succeeded him.

AESTHETICS

the 30-second architecture

RELATED TOPICS
See also
SYMMETRY
page 62

PROPORTION &
THE GOLDEN RATIO
page 76

3-SECOND FOUNDATION
Aesthetics deal with questions of beauty in the arts and nature, as well as the problem of how we judge something as beautiful.

3-MINUTE ELEVATION
Architectural historian Nikolaus Pevsner famously opened his *Outline of European Architecture* (1943) by claiming that while a "bicycle shed is a building; Lincoln Cathedral is a piece of architecture." He goes on to argue that only those buildings that are "designed with a view to aesthetic appeal" qualify to be called architecture. In these terms, architecture must show the potential—and intention—to be judged as beautiful.

The term aesthetics is derived from the Greek for "perceptible" and describes, in its broadest definition, that branch of philosophy concerned with the perception of beauty. During the 18th century, German and British philosophers such as Immanuel Kant and Edmund Burke began to separate sensory appreciation of beauty from reason and intellect. The idea of taste as a distinct mental faculty that determines aesthetic judgment gave rise to influential aesthetic ideals, and the concept of the "sublime and beautiful" was introduced by Burke to distinguish between objects and ideas triggering feelings of terror and pain from those that evoke calm and controlled pleasure. The idea of the "picturesque," often associated with British artist William Gilpin, responded to these by propagating a gentler standard of taste that relied on variety, irregularity, and an ability to pique imagination. Such aesthetic ideals were applied throughout the arts, including sculpture, architecture, literature, painting, and, importantly, landscape design. In architecture, aesthetic judgment can be complicated by the fact that buildings are designed to be functional and not only aesthetically stimulating, unlike other forms of visual art, such as painting or sculpture. In architecture, function and beauty are today often seen as potentially conflicting principles.

3-SECOND BIOGRAPHIES
EDMUND BURKE
1729–97
British philosopher and author of *A Philosophical Enquiry into the Origin of our Ideas of the Sublime and Beautiful* (1757)

IMMANUEL KANT
1724–1804
German philosopher and the first to argue that the sense of beauty is a distinct faculty of the human mind

WILLIAM GILPIN
1724–1804
English artist and one of the originators of the picturesque

30-SECOND TEXT
Anne Hultzsch

Ornamentation is used to trigger an aesthetic effect in the viewer, based on the specific leitmotif of its place and time.

HISTORICISM

the 30-second architecture

RELATED TOPICS
See also
REVIVALISM
page 102

CLASSICISM
page 98

THE RENAISSANCE
page 100

3-SECOND FOUNDATION
The term "historicism" refers to architectural styles that make reference to, and sometimes imitate, historical buildings from the past.

3-MINUTE ELEVATION
Modernists in particular often use the term "historicism" pejoratively in order to emphasize the idea that historicist styles copy and imitate, rather than create. Modernism, in fact, consciously defined itself through a rejection of all literal historical references and ornamentation. The wish to create a new and better world gave rise to the idea that a serious disruption of historical continuity was needed in order to construct a truly new style.

In architecture, historicism refers to building styles that have their origins in the past through an imitation or reinterpretation of historical styles. It begins with the revival of Classical Greek and Roman arts and literature in the Renaissance from the 14th century onward, and continues over the great period of Revivalism in the 18th and 19th centuries up to Postmodern Historicism in the late 20th century. Often triggered by the rediscovery of writings, drawings, or indeed buildings of a past style, historicism stands in close relation to antiquarian and archaeological practices. Alberti's *De Re Aedificatoria* (*On the Art of Building*, 1452), which laid out the ancient orders and thus the foundations for Renaissance architecture, for example, was based on the only surviving ancient treatise on architecture, that by Vitruvius. In the mid-18th century a similar rise in an archaeological study of the Middle Ages and their way of life, often referred to as Romanticism and accompanied by meticulous surveys of medieval architecture, particularly the cathedrals, led to the Gothic Revival. The 19th century is now regarded as the period that reveled in revivals, from Greek and Gothic to Byzantine, Early Christian, Romanesque, Italianate, Elizabethan, Tudor, or Jacobean.

3-SECOND BIOGRAPHIES
LEON BATTISTA ALBERTI
1404–72
Italian humanist writer, who revived classical architectural theory

A. W. N. PUGIN
1812–52
British architect and theorist of the Gothic Revival

JOHANN WINCKELMANN
1717–68
German archaeologist and art historian, who greatly influenced the revival of Classical Greek architecture

30-SECOND TEXT
Anne Hultzsch

Historicist buildings copy or interpret key precedents, taking authority from the past.

PAPER ARCHITECTURE

the 30-second architecture

RELATED TOPICS
See also
AVANT-GARDE
page 106

3-SECOND FOUNDATION
"Paper Architecture" is a term used to describe unbuilt, often fantastical, buildings designed to critique accepted practice or suggest new architectural possibilities.

3-MINUTE ELEVATION
Paper Architecture should not be dismissed as designers' indulgences. Like science fiction, it can be read as social commentary or signposting possible futures. The Pompidou Center, Paris, and Lloyd's Building, London, were inspired by the work of Archigram, a group that posited such architectural innovations. Similarly, the work of the Italian Superstudio group in the 1960s and 1970s and films such as *Metropolis* (1927) are commentaries on urbanization and the relationship between architecture and power.

The term "Paper Architecture" can be applied to Utopian, unbuildable, or otherwise imaginary structures, generally conceived to explore an architectural thesis or cultural/political position. The term was used pejoratively in the postwar Soviet Union to describe the work of architects unhappy with the functional aesthetic of the State. In the 1980s, a Moscow-based group of architects chose to exhibit their work under the title "Paper Architects"—this included the quirky and beautifully drawn work of Alexander Brodsky and Ilya Utkin. The term could also be applied to much earlier depictions, however, including Bruegel the Elder's painting *The Tower of Babel* (1563), which shows an imaginary structure being raised to heaven, and Giovanni Battista Piranesi's series of labyrinthine "imaginary prisons" of the mid-18th century. The French Neoclassical architect Étienne-Louis Boullée drew up designs for structures on a gigantic and improbable scale based on vast spheres and other pure forms, and such large-scale Utopian imaginings were echoed in the 20th century with, for example, Frank Lloyd Wright's 1956 proposal for a mile-high skyscraper with atomic-powered elevators and Buckminster Fuller's 1962 suggestion for placing a geodesic dome over midtown Manhattan.

3-SECOND BIOGRAPHIES
ÉTIENNE-LOUIS BOULLÉE
1728–99
French architect and theorist

RICHARD BUCKMINSTER FULLER
1895–1983
American engineer and developer of the geodesic dome

ARCHIGRAM
1960s–
British group of architects that celebrated innovation and technological possibilities

GIOVANNI BATTISTA PIRANESI
1720–78
Italian architect, engineer, and originator of *invenzioni*

30-SECOND TEXT
David Littlefield

Mostly unrealized, or even improbable, paper architecture can inspire later built works; domes by Buckminster Fuller fall into both categories.

Fig.1.

INVENTOR
RICHARD BUCKMINSTER FULLER
BY
ATTORNEY

FIG.1

Fig.2.

Fig.3.

20 PER SPHERE
SPHERICAL ICOSAHEDRON

12 PER SPHERE
SPHERICAL DODECAHEDRON

30 PER SPHERE
SPHERICAL TRICONTAHEDRON

FIG.2

INVENTOR.
RICHARD BUCKMINSTER FULLER
BY
ATTORNEYS.

CRITICAL REGIONALISM

the 30-second architecture

Critical Regionalism is not an architectural style or movement, but an approach that attempts to combine the benefits of progress, such as advances in the technology of materials and practices, with the specifics of the local situation, such as climate, materials, knowledge, or customs. In the words of its chief proponent, Kenneth Frampton, it is "a cross-fertilization between rooted culture on the one hand and universal civilization on the other." Since Alexander Tzonis and Liane Lefaivre first coined the term in 1981, Frampton developed it in response to the homogeneity of modern architecture and as an alternative to what he saw as the superficiality of Postmodernism. It was, therefore, intended to be a call for a more meaningful Modernism that was in harmony with the peculiarities of a specific place. In this sense, Critical Regionalism has been associated with an approach to place-making that emphasizes experience and the *genius loci*, or spirit of the place. Architects identified as working in this way include Alvar Aalto, for example, his Säynätsalo Town Hall (1952) in Finland, Jørn Utzon with the Bagsværd Church, Copenhagen, Denmark (1976), and Glenn Murcutt with a series of houses in Australia, including the Marika Alderton House (1994).

RELATED TOPICS
See also
MODERNISM
page 108

POSTMODERNISM
page 118

3-SECOND BIOGRAPHIES
JØRN UTZON
1918–2008
Danish architect

KENNETH FRAMPTON
1930–
British architectural critic, closely associated with promoting Critical Regionalism

GLENN MURCUTT
1936–
Australian architect

30-SECOND TEXT
Steve Parnell

Utzon's Bagsværd church uses a unique undulating ceiling to provide a naturally lit interior, inside a quite industrial exterior—an example of modern technique applied to specific program.

3-SECOND FOUNDATION
Critical Regionalism is a type of architecture that looks to respond to specific geographical and/ or cultural situations to resist the universalizing tendency of Modernism.

3-MINUTE ELEVATION
The concept of regionalism grew in popularity as Europe decolonized, and can be found in several postwar architectural movements, sharing concerns with the "as found" of the British New Brutalists and Ernesto Rogers's "pre-existing conditions" in Italy. The *Architectural Review*'s "Townscape" campaign was perhaps closest, although it concerned itself with the combination of modernity and vernacular aesthetically. Critical Regionalism is more about how the essence of a place determines the approach to architectural design.

IDEAS/MOVEMENTS

anthroposophist philosophy Philosophical school founded by Rudolf Steiner (1861–1925), which sought knowledge of the spiritual world in a way that is intellectually credible. In architecture, it found expression in the holistic and harmonious concerns of Organic Architecture.

Deconstructivism A style that "deconstructs" and fragments buildings, which developed as a reaction to the straight lines and order of Modernism. Fluidity and a controlled use of surprising forms characterize the style, as exemplified by Frank Gehry's Guggenheim Museum, Bilbao (1997), and the Jewish Museum, Berlin (1999) by Daniel Libeskind.

English Baroque A parallel development in England to Continental Baroque, starting with Sir Christopher Wren—St. Paul's Cathedral in London (1675–1711) is an example—and characterized by a subtle Classicism, less exuberant than many Continental examples. Nicholas Hawksmoor and Sir John Vanbrugh were two other notable practitioners.

Expressionism A development of Art Nouveau and a dominant style in Europe, c. 1905–25. In some ways the antithesis of Functionalism, artistic expression is core to the style, perfectly exemplified by Antoni Gaudí's extraordinary Sagrada Família in Barcelona (begun 1882).

Futurism A movement originating in Italy in 1909 that concerned itself with and glorified modernity, technology, and ideas of the future. Some Futurist buildings were constructed under Mussolini, and the style has been associated with Italian Fascism.

informatics In architecture and planning, a general term for how Information and Communications Technology is used in the creation and management of built environments.

Mannerism Style of art, principally Italian, of c. 1520–1620. Rooted in Classicism, it shows marked characteristics that separate it from Renaissance and Baroque works, including use of distorted and strained human figures—often with marked musculature—and a use of vivid colors.

New Urbanism Movement originating in America in the 1980s—related to the Urban Village movement in Europe—that promotes a form of urban development on a more human, specifically walkable, scale as an antidote to most postwar urban sprawl.

Purism Art movement founded by Amadée Ozenfant and Le Corbusier in 1918 as a reaction to the perceived decorative nature of later Cubism. This stance subsequently found its way into Le Corbusier's architecture.

Unités d'Habitation A concept by Le Corbusier for a "vertical village," all contained within one slab block. The most famous of these is in Marseilles. Surrounded by parkland, it houses 1,600 residents and has an internal shopping street and a recreation ground and kindergarten on the roof.

CLASSICISM

the 30-second architecture

Despite the use of Roman forms

before the Renaissance, it was not until the 16th century that such forms and styles were re-established as the emergent, even dominant, architectural language. Adoption of the Classical orders—Doric, Ionic, Corinthian, Tuscan, and Composite—underpins this movement, in which building structures are composed of vertical and horizontal elements (such as columns, capitals, and entablatures), which conform to precise codes and forms. Classicism moved through various phases —Mannerism, Baroque, Rococo, Palladianism, Neoclassicism, Greek Revival, and Beaux Arts— each adopting a particular position to, or interpretation of, Greek and Roman models. Mannerism and Baroque, for example, display a certain artistic freedom and experimentalism, in contrast to the austerity of mid-17th-century Greek Revival. During this time, architects began to look beyond Renaissance texts and return to source material from antiquity through archaeological explorations at Pompeii and Herculaneum, as well as Greece. Architects of the period (notably Claude-Nicolas Ledoux) also explored the possibilities of pure form, such as the pyramid and the sphere, giving their work an Egyptian flavor. Classical architecture became more opulent during the 19th century, often on a scale designed to evoke the power of Imperial Rome.

3-SECOND FOUNDATION
Classicism is the use of principles and precedents from antiquity in building design, largely to denote ideas of order, harmony, empire, and power.

3-MINUTE ELEVATION
Classicism has long been identified as the architectural language of the state and civic amenities such as banks, museums, and railway stations. Karl Friedrich Schinkel used Classicism to monumental effect in Prussia in the 19th century, and the firm of McKim, Mead & White—arguably one of the foremost proponents of Neoclassicism in the U.S.—produced major works, including the now-demolished Pennsylvania Station in New York, based on the Baths of Caracalla in Rome.

RELATED TOPICS
See also
CLASSICAL GREECE
page 18

ROMAN
page 20

THE COLUMN
page 46

SYMMETRY
page 62

RENAISSANCE
page 100

3-SECOND BIOGRAPHIES
SIR CHRISTOPHER WREN
1632–1723
English architect and leader of the English Baroque

CLAUDE-NICOLAS LEDOUX
1736–1806
Prominent French Neoclassicist, few of whose works survive

30-SECOND TEXT
David Littlefield

Classicism deploys the architectural devices of Greece and Rome. The dome and rounded arch are Roman innovations not seen in Greek works.

THE RENAISSANCE

the 30-second architecture

RELATED TOPICS
See also
CLASSICISM
page 98

BAROQUE
page 124

3-SECOND FOUNDATION
The term "Renaissance" refers to the flourishing of the arts during the 15th and 16th centuries— embracing architecture, sculpture, painting, and the idea of perfection.

3-MINUTE ELEVATION
As well as characterizing the design of individual buildings, Renaissance ideas influenced urban design and planning. In 1458 Pope Pius II ordered the reconstruction of his birthplace, Pienza, based on Renaissance values. Arguably the only town entirely laid out along geometrically pure lines is Valetta in Malta, designed by Francesco Laparelli in 1566. Piero della Francesca's painting *The Ideal City* (c. 1470) is a powerful expression of this vision of urban purity.

"Renaissance," meaning rebirth, is the name given to the cultural movement that had its earliest beginnings around the time of Giotto (c. 1266–1337), lasting through to Raphael (1483–1520) and Palladio (1508–1580). The movement began as a northern Italian phenomenon, centered on the city states of Florence and Siena. The Renaissance was funded by increased wealth and trade, which made the role of patrons such as the Church and powerful families, including the Medici, very important. Significantly, this era marked a break with traditional medieval and Gothic architecture, described by contemporary writer Vasari as "barbaric." Instead, artists and architects (who often performed both roles) began to study the remains of the Classical past—Brunelleschi, for example, spent long periods measuring and drawing the relics of Rome. Buildings began to feature rounded arches, domes, triangular pediments, and Classical columns. Further, buildings (in plan and elevation) came to be composed through geometrically pure shapes, such as squares and circles in an attempt to convey a sense of harmony, and—even—perfection. Such techniques were accompanied by the discovery of the mathematics of perspective, allowing paintings and depictions of buildings to convey a lifelike sense of depth.

3-SECOND BIOGRAPHIES
FILIPPO BRUNELLESCHI
1377–1446
Architect and sculptor; architect of the cupola (dome) atop the cathedral in Florence

MICHELANGELO BUONARROTI
1475–1564
Artist, sculptor, and architect of the Laurentian Library, the Palazzo Farnese, and the Porta Pia

LEON BATTISTA ALBERTI
1404–72
Architect and architectural theorist

30-SECOND TEXT
David Littlefield

Renaissance architects deployed Classical features and pure geometric forms to create an impression of harmony.

REVIVALISM

the 30-second architecture

The first important revival in the West was the Italian Renaissance in the 14th century, which revived Classical Greek and Roman architecture. The Renaissance itself later inspired multiple revivals, such as Palladianism in Britain. Greek Revival architecture became popular in the mid-18th century—with Claude-Nicolas Ledoux in France, Sir John Soane in England, and Thomas Jefferson in the USA as early proponents—peaking in the early 19th century. This took inspiration from the simplicity and severity of the Doric temple that contrasts starkly with later Roman forms. Even earlier, the Gothic Revival emerged in the 18th century with an accurate use of medieval forms, such as the pointed arch, the rib vault, or glazed windows. In the 19th century, the choice of styles turned into a veritable battle when A. W. N. Pugin ascribed the Gothic with superior moral and religious ideals derived from a romantic interpretation of medieval life. At its height in the 19th century, the Gothic was applied to an increasing number of public buildings, including London's Palace of Westminster (Sir Charles Barry and A. W. N. Pugin, 1865), the Town Hall in Vienna (Friedrich von Schmidt, 1883), and the Rijksmuseum in Amsterdam (Pierre Cuypers, 1871).

3-SECOND FOUNDATION
Revivalist architecture denotes those buildings that take inspiration from, or reinterpret, past architectural styles, a paradigm that was particularly popular in the 19th century.

3-MINUTE ELEVATION
Early in the Revivalist period, when style became a matter of choice, the variety of styles led to some bizarre stylistic combinations within the same building: in Nicholas Hawksmoor's All Souls College, Oxford (1740), for example, Gothic was chosen for the exterior and Baroque for the interior. In the 19th century, such stylistic medleys became characteristic of eclectic buildings such as Joseph Poelaert's Palace of Justice in Brussels (1883), which presents Neoclassical and Gothic elements.

RELATED TOPICS
See also
GOTHIC
page 28

HISTORICISM
page 88

3-SECOND BIOGRAPHIES
NICHOLAS HAWKSMOOR
1661–1736
English architect, who developed his own Baroque style from Classical and Gothic elements

THOMAS JEFFERSON
1743–1826
Third American president, and self-taught architect who introduced the Greek Revival style to the USA

SIR JOHN SOANE
1753–1837
English architect and one of the most important proponents and interpreters of Neoclassicism

30-SECOND TEXT
Anne Hultzsch

Architects revive the spirit of a past age in both parts as well as the composition of their designs.

ARTS & CRAFTS

the 30-second architecture

RELATED TOPICS
See also
GOTHIC
page 28

FORM FOLLOWS FUNCTION
page 78

3-SECOND FOUNDATION
The Arts & Crafts movement began in mid-Victorian Britain in reaction to industrial and commercial advancements, and celebrated craft production of decorative arts and architecture.

3-MINUTE ELEVATION
The Arts & Crafts movement was motivated most of all by a desire to change the way buildings were made. Industrial production had resulted in a split between the designer deciding on the look of a building, and the contractor (building firm) deciding how and with what it would be built. For many in the Arts & Crafts world, the ideal would be for the architect and the builder to be one and the same.

Arts & Crafts architecture is characterized by a number of vernacular features, as Arts & Crafts architects consciously chose to highlight local traditions in their work—low, pitched roofs, decorative brickwork, tall chimneys, irregular patterns of windows and doors, and mixtures of different kinds of material, including wood, stone, brick, tile, lead, iron, and thatch. These were not only stylistic effects, but also the result of two key principles: that the designer should collaborate with the builder, relying on and supporting the builder's knowledge of materials and craft techniques; and that the resulting building should be comfortable and fit within its immediate landscape. The most celebrated examples of Arts & Crafts architecture are domestic homes, which were organized around a communal core—the hearth and inglenook, a semi-enclosed seating area around a fireplace. The interiors appear casual and comfortable, and the building and furniture demonstrate the handcrafting of the materials used. Beginning in Britain, the Arts & Crafts movement had an international influence. German designers were particularly interested in the domestic designs, but the most enthusiastic take-up was in North America, where Arts & Crafts principles fitted neatly with ideals of nature, landscape, and community.

3-SECOND BIOGRAPHIES
WILLIAM MORRIS
1834–96
British socialist, designer, and leading theorist of the Arts & Crafts movement

WILLIAM R. LETHABY
1857–1931
British architect and art historian, cofounder of the Art Workers Guild and a leading practitioner of Arts & Crafts

CHARLES SUMNER GREENE & HENRY MATHER GREENE
1868–1957 & 1870–1954
Influential American Arts & Crafts architects

30-SECOND TEXT
Nick Beech

Arts & Crafts homes are total works of art—from the walls through timber frames to rugs and wallpaper design.

ATTIC

SHIPLAP

TRAP DOOR

2" X 6" JOISTS 24" O.C.

BRACE

STAIR HALL

BATH ROOM

WOOD FLOOR

PORCH

2 3/4 X 9" JOIST 24" O.C.

LIVING ROOM

KITCHEN

SOLID CEDAR POSTS

WOOD FLOOR

STONE FLOOR

AVANT-GARDE

the 30-second architecture

3-SECOND FOUNDATION
The "avant-garde" is literally the foremost part of a military advance, but used culturally, it refers to artists or works that are innovative or experimental.

3-MINUTE ELEVATION
The "neo-avant-garde" refers to postwar groups such as the New Brutalists and Archigram in Britain, and the Metabolists in Japan, which, while progressive, were not revolutionary like their predecessors. Some argue that the Avant-garde is an inherent characteristic of Modernism, and the generator of progress through a dialectic process of initially existing and ultimately becoming intrinsic to the mainstream. Avant-garde architects are often identified more by their manifestos than by their built work.

Avant-garde architecture includes the factions of architects that reject mainstream ideas and push the boundaries of conventional architectural thinking. Historically this refers to a number of iconoclastic European groups and individuals at the beginning of the 20th century, who forged a new architecture more appropriate for the machine age than the complacent bourgeois values, institutions, and style wars of traditional art and architecture. Modern architecture developed from these progressive ideas, among which the most important early groups were the Futurists immediately before World War I and the Constructivists immediately after. Futurism emphasized speed, technology, violence, the aestheticization of the machine, mass industrialization, and war, while the Constructivists argued for the unification of art and life through its use to promote social and political progress. In the early volatile years of the 1900s, art was infused with politics, and Futurism became associated with Fascism in Italy and Constructivism with Communism in the USSR. Although, like Vladimir Tatlin's Monument to the Third International (1919), such Avant-garde architecture mostly only ever appeared on paper or as models, both movements became hugely influential on later progressive ones including De Stijl in Holland and the Bauhaus in Germany.

RELATED TOPICS
See also
MODERNISM
page 108

METABOLISM
page 114

3-SECOND BIOGRAPHIES
ANTONIO SANT'ELIA
1888–1916
Influential Italian Futurist architect who envisioned the Città Nuova (1912–14), which only ever appeared on paper

VLADIMIR TATLIN
1885–1953
Russian/Soviet Constructivist architect and designer of the seminal Monument to the Third International (1919)

30-SECOND TEXT
Steve Parnell

Russian Constructivism was one of the most progressive movements of the avant-garde, producing unadorned, geometric structures, inspired by engineering.

MODERNISM

the 30-second architecture

Architectural Modernism embraces
a multitude of 20th-century movements that
share stylistic and technical characteristics, such
as abstraction, mass production, industrialization,
scientific rationalization, universalization, rejection
of tradition, and a general belief in "form follows
function." In the 1920s, a number of avant-garde
movements invented new ways of building for
the machine age that sought to use technology
to improve everybody's everyday life. Italian
Rationalism developed an undecorated and
logical but classical modern architecture, Russian
Constructivism aimed to unite art and life through
an expression of architectural elements, Dutch de
Stijl and French Purism strove to transpose Cubist
painting to architecture, and the German Bauhaus
sought to marry industrial production with good
design. Modern architecture became known in the
USA as International Style after a 1932 exhibition
showing the new European architecture. It
attained almost universal acceptance for postwar
reconstruction due to its speed, scale, and relative
inexpensiveness, and remains the dominant
design idiom. Its most influential protagonist was
arguably Le Corbusier, whose writings, ideas, and
buildings—key among them the Villa Savoye, Paris
(1931), various Unités d'Habitation housing blocks,
and the city of Chandigarh, India (1959)—have
influenced generations of architects.

3-SECOND FOUNDATION
Modernism is the cultural
and artistic manifestation
of modernity, and it
dominated 20th-century
thought, promoting
progress toward a better
future through scientific
rationalization.

3-MINUTE ELEVATION
"Modern" should
not be confused
with "contemporary"
architecture—Modernism
is a set of ideas and
world views that reject
history and are associated
with progress. It is a moot
point whether Modernism
has been replaced or
merely extended by
Postmodernism. The motif
that arguably exemplifies
modern architecture as a
style and simultaneously
exposes its contradictions
is the flat roof, which
completely fails in terms of
form following function.

RELATED TOPICS
See also
FORM FOLLOWS FUNCTION
page 78

AVANT-GARDE
page 106

POSTMODERNISM
page 118

INTERNATIONAL STYLE
page 130

3-SECOND BIOGRAPHIES
LE CORBUSIER
1887–1965
Swiss-born architect most
closely associated with and
influential on Modernism

WALTER GROPIUS
1883–1969
German-born architect and
founder of the Bauhaus, who
later worked in the USA

30-SECOND TEXT
Steve Parnell

The Unité d'Habitation is
a Modernist architecture
icon. Seen as a village
within one building, it
was highly influential
on postwar housing.

ORGANIC ARCHITECTURE

the 30-second architecture

3-SECOND FOUNDATION
Organic architecture
strives to create a unified,
harmonic, interrelated
whole of buildings and
environment, and it
synthesizes form and
function independently
from style.

3-MINUTE ELEVATION
The term "Organic
Architecture" was coined
by Frank Lloyd Wright to
describe his approach to
buildings as organisms
with all-inclusive designs,
where every element—
from layout and technical
details to windows,
ornamentation to
furniture—relates to
every other. One famous
example is the Fallingwater
house in Pennsylvania
(1935), which he positioned
directly over a waterfall to
create a dialogue between
the steep site and the large
horizontal cantilevered
terraces of the house.

Unlike the more regular geometry
of most architectural idioms, organic
architecture takes its inspiration from natural
forms. The Arts & Crafts and Art Nouveau
movements of the late 19th century display
some of its concerns: a desire to use local
materials, a commitment to handcrafting rather
than mass-produced uniformity, and flowing,
asymmetrical forms that harmonize with
surrounding natural features. New technologies
in metalwork and concrete allowed this to
develop: the plantlike curves and tendrils of
Art Nouveau could be realized in wrought
iron—as in Hector Guimard's Paris Metro station
entrances—while Erich Mendelsohn's Einstein
Tower at Potsdam employed concrete to create
a curvaceous, sculptural form. Key early figures
include Frank Lloyd Wright and Louis Sullivan in
America and Hugo Häring, Rudolf Steiner, and
Hans Scharoun in Europe. After the mid-20th
century, the concept of organic architecture was
taken to new Expressionistic heights, including
the freeformed Sydney Opera House by Jørn
Utzon (1973; designed 1957) and the TWA Flight
Center at JFK International Airport, New York
(1962), as well as to futuristic designs based
on cybernetic and informatic models of life
as researched by Buckminster Fuller, and the
contemporary move toward biomimetic design.

RELATED TOPICS
See also
ARTS & CRAFTS
page 104

ART NOUVEAU
page 128

BIOMIMETICS
page 148

3-SECOND BIOGRAPHIES
RUDOLF STEINER
1861–1925
Austrian anthroposophist
philosopher, architect, writer

BRUCE GOFF
1904–1982
American architect, well
known for his idiosyncratic,
eclectic, organic architecture

IMRE MAKOVECZ
1935–2011
Hungarian architect and
prominent proponent of
organic architecture

30-SECOND TEXT
Marjan Colletti

*Architecture has
always appealed to
nature's organic
functions and forms
for inspiration.*

June 8, 1867
Born Frank Lincoln Wright—he took Lloyd from his mother's maiden name after his father deserted the family—in Richland Center, Wisconsin

1886–7
Attended the University of Wisconsin-Madison

1887
Worked for architect Joseph Silsbee in Chicago

1888–93
Worked for Dankmar Adler and Louis Sullivan

1893
Established his own practice in Chicago

1893
First independent commission, the Winslow House, River Forest, Illinois

1900–2
Built the first four houses that introduced the principles of what became known as the Prairie School

1905–8
Built the Unity Temple, Oak Park, Illinois

1908–10
Built the Robie House, Chicago

1911
Began work on a house, Taliesin, at Spring Green, Wisconsin. It was burned down in 1914

1915
Designed the Imperial Hotel, Tokyo

1926–31
Designed the Graycliff Estate, Buffalo, New York

1932
Opened the rebuilt Taliesin

1935
Designed the iconic Fallingwater, Pennsylvania

1936–7
Built the Jacobs House, the first Usonian House

1936
Worked on the Johnson Wax Research Tower, Racine, Wisconsin

1937
Moved to Phoenix, Arizona, and built Taliesin West

1943
Began designing the Solomon R. Guggenheim Museum, New York,

1952–6
Built the Price Tower, Bartlesville, Oklahoma

1959
Opening of his last project, the Kalita Humphreys Theater, Dallas, Texas

April 9, 1959
Died in Phoenix, Arizona

FRANK LLOYD WRIGHT

Acknowledged as one of the greatest American architects of all time, Frank Lloyd Wright—architect, interior designer, writer, educator, father of Organic Architecture, leader of the Prairie School, advocate and creator of Usonian housing, pioneer of open-plan living—led a long, successful, and prolific career. He produced more than 1,000 designs, of which over half were realized, and created in his masterpiece, Fallingwater, an iconic piece of Americana and the architectural equivalent of the Great American Novel.

Wright started work in Chicago, aged 20, expertly networking his mother's influential family. He was soon employed by Dankmar Adler and Louis Sullivan, and he was greatly influenced by Sullivan's ideas, but famously fell out with him when caught moonlighting on other buildings to supplement his income.

Wright went on to lead what became known as the Prairie School, whose signature designs used unpainted organic materials, low-lying horizontal structures, wraparound windows, a central hearth, and open-plan space inside. He also designed furniture, fittings, and window glass for his houses, so presenting a unified whole. Wright's buildings expressed themselves through organic structure and the mimicking of natural forms, as well as through the building's materials and setting.

The Price Tower (1952–6), in Bartlesville, Oklahoma, for example, is based on the form of a tree, with the services carried in a central trunk and the rooms cantilevered out on branches, while the helical Solomon R. Guggenheim Museum (opened in 1959) crouches like an enormous snail in central New York.

After the horrific murder of his mistress Martha Cheney, her children, and five others and the burning of their home, Taliesin, in 1914 Wright went to Japan, commissioned to build the Imperial Hotel, Tokyo. He was greatly inspired by Japanese art and the use of simple materials and landscaping, which is apparent in his designs for the Graycliff Estate (1926–31). He rebuilt Taliesin (twice), and in 1932 opened it up as an architectural studio. Here he created the concept for Broadacre City, several Usonian houses, the Johnson Wax Research Tower in Racine, Wisconsin (1944–51), and Fallingwater. In 1937 he built Taliesin West in Scottsdale, Arizona, establishing the Frank Lloyd Wright Foundation there and designing the Solomon R. Guggenheim Museum, the Price Tower, various community housing schemes and Usonian homes, and his last work, the Kalita Humphreys Theater, Dallas (opened 1959).

Claiming few influences himself, Frank Lloyd Wright has had a truly profound effect on subsequent architects.

METABOLISM

the 30-second architecture

The Metabolists announced themselves with the manifesto *Metabolism: The Proposals for New Urbanism* at the 1960 World Design Conference in Tokyo. This proposed a number of ideas for future cities by architect members of the group, including Kisho Kurokawa and Kiyonori Kikutake. The Metabolists rejected the influential mechanistic way of thinking about reconstructing postwar cities advocated by CIAM (Congrès Internationaux d'Architecture Moderne), suggesting more biological metaphors that allowed for impermanence, portability, and improved flexibility. Technology remained an enabler, but at its root was the idea of the city as a process. Many of the group's proposals involved building megastructures on the sea or huge towers in the sky, often with biomorphic imagery. The Tokyo Bay Plan (1960) by Kenzo Tange, who mentored the group but was never a member himself, is an early example of such a vast floating infrastructure of buildings and highways spanning the bay. The individual capsule was also a recurring motif that featured as an easily replaceable minimalist inhabitable unit within a larger framework. One of the few built examples of Metabolist architecture is Kisho Kurokawa's Nakagin Capsule Tower (1972), composed of capsules designed to last only 25 years on a more permanent core.

3-SECOND FOUNDATION
Metabolism was a Japanese movement that envisioned cities as living organisms, comprising elements with different metabolic cycles that transformed over time.

3-MINUTE ELEVATION
The group's swan song was the 1970 Tokyo Expo, which Tange masterplanned and invited Metabolists to contribute buildings. They constructed many impressive pavilions and structures, but the social ideas of the movement were lost to the inevitable consumerist and exhibitionist nature of an event intended to promote modern Japanese design and technology. The future of the Nakagin Capsule Tower is currently being debated, provoked more by property prices than by questions of architectural merit.

RELATED TOPICS
See also
MODERNISM
page 108

AVANT-GARDE
page 106

3-SECOND BIOGRAPHIES
KENZO TANGE
1913–2005
Arguably Japan's most celebrated architect and mentor of Metabolist group

KISHO KUROKAWA
1934–2007
Japanese architect, founding member of the Metabolists, and designer of the Nakagin Capsule Tower

30-SECOND TEXT
Steve Parnell

The Nakagin Capsule Tower is a rare example of built Metabolist architecture. Its prefabricated capsules fitted to a permanent core were intended to be reconfigured or replaced over time.

HIGH-TECH

the 30-second architecture

A key characteristic of High-tech architecture is its use of metal and glass. In aesthetic terms it proposes a form of inverted approach, in which the honesty of expression, even in terms of revealing the bones and internal structure of the building, is regarded as desirable. This approach embodies ideas about industrial and mass production that can—although not always—allow elements of the building to be standardized and produced in a factory, before assembly on site. One of the priorities of High-tech is flexibility of use, which means that the emphasis is on functionality of space rather than its social or artistic privileges, exemplified by Richard Rogers and Renzo Piano's Pompidou Center in Paris. High-tech buildings are therefore designed to be efficient and functional, rather than serving a specific purpose. As Le Corbusier described the house as "a machine for living," but struggled to achieve this kind of aesthetic fully, High-tech exemplifies the potential of this maxim. In High-tech architecture, the "machine" is a metaphor that depicts applied technology and serves as a source of inspiration and imagery. Such buildings relate little to their context, and their aesthetics do not reflect what goes on inside the building.

RELATED TOPICS
See also
PAPER ARCHITECTURE
page 90

MODERNISM
page 108

POSTMODERNISM
page 118

CAD
page 142

3-SECOND BIOGRAPHIES
SIR NORMAN FOSTER
1935–
British architect, one of the pioneers of High-tech architecture in Britain

RENZO PIANO
1937–
Italian architect, codesigner (with Richard Rogers) of the Pompidou Center, Paris, and architect of the Shard, London

30-SECOND TEXT
Dragana Cebzan Antic

3-SECOND FOUNDATION
Emerging in the early 1970s, High-tech architecture employs the latest construction methods and technologies, including prefabrication and standardization, creating a structural and functional aesthetic.

3-MINUTE ELEVATION
Two common attributes of High-tech architecture are the use of exposed structure and open services. The underlying aesthetic is seen in the expressive quality of the structure with the extensive use of steel as a structural framework or supporting device. Steel, as well as steel reinforced concrete, is favored because of its high tensile strength, which allows for structural lightness and functional open-plan interiors.

The honesty of the façade materials is a recognizable quality of High-tech architecture.

POSTMODERNISM

the 30-second architecture

The critic Charles Jencks, father of the Anglo-American strain of Postmodernism, asserted that "Modern architecture died in St. Louis, Missouri, on July 15, 1972 at 3.32pm," when the unloved Pruitt-Igoe slab-housing blocks were demolished. Postmodernism should be deemed more a sensibility than an individual style or movement, as it comprises various movements, including Pluralism and Deconstructivism, all of which are resistant to Modernist dogma. The height of Postmodern architecture was 1977–92, when it was mainly concerned with questions of taste and architecture's ability to communicate with the general public, as well as an architectural elite (its so-called "double-coding"). Robert Venturi and Denise Scott Brown in *Learning from Las Vegas* (1972) discuss this at length in an attempt to show that the advertising of Las Vegas Strip was "almost all right." Other communication devices are the use of historical references, often in irony or as parody, and a reliance on the façade to communicate with no reference to a building's internal layout. Seminal Postmodern works include Michael Graves's Portland Building, Portland, Oregon (1982), Philip Johnson's AT&T Building, New York (1984), and James Stirling's Staatsgalerie, Stuttgart (1984). The New Urbanism of Leon Krier at Seaside, Florida, and Poundbury, Dorchester, UK, are also considered Postmodern.

3-SECOND FOUNDATION
Postmodernism was a direct response to the alienation and growing disillusionment with modern architecture that both architects and the public felt in the late 1960s.

3-MINUTE ELEVATION
Postmodern architecture is considered by purists as lacking taste, two-dimensional, regressive, or even downright dishonest. However, the recent popularity of iconic buildings can be seen as a continuation of a Postmodern desire to communicate. Throughout the 1980s, Postmodernism quickly became associated with the interests of big business, such as Michael Graves's work at Disneyland, Paris, and César Pelli at Docklands, London, so the label was disowned for selling out to commercialism.

RELATED TOPICS
See also
CRITICAL REGIONALISM
page 92

MODERNISM
page 108

3-SECOND BIOGRAPHIES
ROBERT VENTURI & DENISE SCOTT BROWN
1925– & 1931–
American architects who studied and wrote on architectural coding

MICHAEL GRAVES
1934–
American architect deemed to be associated with architectural "Disneyfication"

CHARLES JENCKS
1939–
Anglo-American architectural critic, author of *The Language of Post-Modern Architecture*

30-SECOND TEXT
Steve Parnell

The AT&T (now Sony) Building, New York and the Portland Building, Oregon, are seminal Postmodern buildings.

STYLES

Chinoiserie Imitation of or influence by Chinese artforms, first appearing in the 17th century and lasting into the 19th. Architecturally this was expressed in landscaping, teahouses, pavilions, and pagodas, notably the Great Pagoda, Kew Gardens, London (1759).

Enlightenment Also the Age of Enlightenment/Reason, this was an intellectual movement beginning in the late 17th century and lasting into the 18th, dedicated to the advancement of knowledge and the reform of society on "enlightened" lines.

Hindoo style A form of Orientalism, principally, although not exclusively, in Britain that found favor during the 19th century as European involvement in India widened. It makes use of Indian motifs and detailing, and can be seen in such buildings as the Royal Pavilion, Brighton, UK (1823). Can also refer to the Indo-Gothic architecture of British architects in India, which mixed indigenous elements with imported Gothic Revival, as exemplified by the Chhatrapati Shivaji (formerly Victoria) Terminus, Mumbai (1888).

in-situ concrete One of two methods of fabricating reinforced concrete for slab building, the in-situ concrete method is when the liquid concrete is poured into forms on the building site, that is, "in situ." The second method, precast concrete, is where building components are manufactured off-site and transported ready-made to the building site for assembly.

Independent Group An interdisciplinary group of British artists and architects that challenged the Modernist hegemony of the day and advocated a fusion of popular and high art and culture, adopting an "as found" philosophy. They took a radical approach to visual culture, using sources ranging from science-fiction magazines to Hollywood to the work of Abstract Expressionist painter Jackson Pollock. The principal architectural contributions came from the husband-and-wife team of Alison and Peter Smithson.

Japonism A form of Orientalism popular in the 19th century that found inspiration in Japanese artforms. In architecture, Japanese influence can be seen in the work of the likes of Charles Rennie Mackintosh in Scotland and Frank Lloyd Wright in America.

Jugendstil "Young style," the German name for Art Nouveau.

Modernismo The Spanish name for Art Nouveau—also known as Modernisme in Catalan, Barcelona being the main center of the movement in Spain, particularly the works of Antoni Gaudí.

Orientalism A broad term used in the history of art and architecture to describe Western artworks that show influences from the Orient—which could mean anywhere ranging from the Middle East right through to Japan. In architecture, the Hindoo style started to be seen in the late 18th century, and other styles included Chinoiserie, Japonism, Turquerie, Egyptian Revival, and Indo-Gothic. The term has acquired more negative connotations in recent decades, particularly since Edward Saïd's 1978 book *Orientalism*, which saw it as a symptom of Western imperialism rooted in "exoticism" and notions of cultural superiority.

postcolonial theory An exploration of how the world—and in particular previously colonized peoples and their former imperial rulers—can progress in a postcolonial era, culturally and politically, on a more equal basis. See also Orientalism.

Stile Floreale "Floral style," the Italian name for Art Nouveau. Also known as Stile Liberty after Liberty & Co., a department store in London whose designers helped to popularize the style.

sunburst An ornamental motif in which "rays" burst out from a central disk, so resembling sunbeams. Found in Baroque architecture and also a feature of Art Nouveau and Art Deco.

Team X Group of architects that first assembled at the ninth CIAM conference in 1953, eventually presiding over its demise in 1959. Gave rise both to the New Brutalism movement in Britain and to the Structuralists in the Netherlands.

BAROQUE

the 30-second architecture

The Baroque was a development of Classicism in which the rules of ancient precedent became subject to highly inventive, even organic, treatment. Michelangelo was one of the first to play with the elements of Roman architecture, subverting them in a style now known as Mannerism, but the Baroque adopted a more fluid language than earlier styles, deploying ellipses, interpenetrating curves, optical illusions, and other complex geometries. Beginning in Italy, the style reached central Europe (Bavaria and Bohemia especially), France, Spain, and Spain's South American colonies. It appeared in England, largely through the work of Wren and Hawksmoor, but the inventiveness of even these architects is eclipsed by the theatricality and daring of the Italians Francesco Borromini and Giovanni Lorenzo Bernini. Bernini is perhaps best known for his sculpture *The Ecstasy of Saint Theresa* (1652), but his elliptical church Sant'Andrea al Quirinale (1670) in Rome is one of his finest achievements. His contemporary Borromini explored the architectural possibilities of complex mathematics, including the counterpointing of convex/concave to create an impression of movement. The Baroque triggered the 18th-century Rococo style, which added scrollwork and marine motifs such as shells to the palette of decorative elements.

3-SECOND FOUNDATION
The term Baroque describes the exuberant architectural and sculptural styles of the 17th–18th centuries, where formalism became replaced by freer expression and experimentation.

3-MINUTE ELEVATION
The Baroque is not confined to the period of the Enlightenment, as it made a brief reappearance in Britain between around 1890 and 1910 in what some call the "Wrenaissance." It could also be argued that the spirit of the period's aesthetic and structural inventiveness can be seen in the work of Spain's Antoni Gaudí and even the work of today's architects, using computer-generated parametric design tools to evolve complex, fluid, and daring forms.

RELATED TOPICS
See also
AESTHETICS
page 86

CLASSICISM
page 98

THE RENAISSANCE
page 100

3-SECOND BIOGRAPHIES
GIOVANNI LORENZO BERNINI
1598–1680
Italian sculptor, architect, and painter key to the development of Roman Baroque

FRANCESCO BORROMINI
1599–1667
Italian Baroque architect concerned with geometric intricacies

NICHOLAS HAWKSMOOR
1661–1736
English Baroque architect

30-SECOND TEXT
David Littlefield

Baroque architecture adds an experimental, and often complex, exuberance to Classical precedents.

ORIENTALISM

the 30-second architecture

Orientalism grew from the exploration of the Middle East and Asia by Europeans. Artifacts and stories brought back from afar excited a curiosity and hunger in Europe for these mysterious cultures. Different Asian styles have often been highly fashionable, appearing in various forms of cultural and artistic expression throughout Europe for centuries. Painters, textile designers, potters, furniture makers, and architects incorporated the imagery and styles of the Orient into their work. There were various sources from which Western architects found inspiration, but trade and empire made India, China, and, later, Japan the most important. Chinoiserie, the Chinese strand within Orientalism, was most popular in the mid-18th century, with Japonism, Japanese-influenced designs, a century later. The "Hindoo style" remained a popular architectural reference throughout much of the 19th century. Architecturally, Orientalism can be seen in the adoption of all kinds of ornate features, from towering minarets to upturned eaves. Notable English examples include the Great Pagoda in Kew Gardens (1759), London, designed by Sir William Chambers, the Royal Pavilion (1823) in Brighton by John Nash for the Prince Regent, and, in the USA, Gamble House (1909) by Greene & Greene in California.

3-SECOND FOUNDATION
As a style, Orientalism took inspiration from the panoply of "exotic" cultures of the East—once known as the Orient—from North Africa to Japan.

3-MINUTE ELEVATION
Orientalism's popularity has fluctuated over time. It experienced a brief renaissance in the 1930s, and even inspired great Modernists such as Frank Lloyd Wright. However, many commentators have been highly disparaging. Writers Horace Walpole (1717–97) and William Mason (1725–97) vehemently criticized Chambers's chinoiserie, and today Orientalism is associated in a largely negative way with the postcolonial theory expounded by the intellectual Edward Saïd dealing with the West's exploitation of the East.

RELATED TOPICS
See also
ART DECO
page 132

MODERNISM
page 108

3-SECOND BIOGRAPHIES
SIR WILLIAM CHAMBERS
1723–96
British architect and a champion of chinoiserie

SAMUEL PEPYS COCKERELL
1754–1827
British architect

FRANK LLOYD WRIGHT
1867–1959
American architect famously inspired by Japanese design

30-SECOND TEXT
Edward Denison

Inspired by decorative forms in the manifold cultures from north Africa to the far East, Orientalism found expression in art, crafts, design, and architecture.

ART NOUVEAU

the 30-second architecture

RELATED TOPICS
See also
ARTS & CRAFTS
page 104

MODERNISM
page 108

ORGANIC ARCHITECTURE
page 110

3-SECOND FOUNDATION
Art Nouveau was a style of decorative arts and architecture inspired by nature and employing curvaceous organic forms and lines that flourished from 1890–1910.

3-MINUTE ELEVATION
Art Nouveau is often interpreted either as a decorative style (one that has had no influence on modern architecture) or an artistic movement that emerged from specific cultural and temporal contexts. Either way, Art Nouveau's variety of different aesthetic approaches, from formal geometric structures to looser naturalistic forms and patterns, suggests it transcended mere stylistic concerns and represented a legitimate expression of architecture.

The term "Art Nouveau" (as the style became known in Belgium, France, Britain, and the USA) first appeared in 1904 as the title for a collection of essays by professional architects, artists, and craftsmen published by the London periodical *The Magazine of Art*. The main attributes of Art Nouveau's colorful architectural language can be seen in the architectural elements and fittings that were applied to buildings—including doors, windows, wall applications, railings, and banisters—rather than a building's structure. The style was also known as Jugendstil in Germany, Austria, and Scandinavia, Modernismo in Spain, and Stile Floreale in Italy, all of which reflect the vibrant, playful, and floral elements that it displayed. Among the influences on the development of Art Nouveau architecture were the 19th-century emphasis on "new" materials such as iron and glass, but also the desirability of making structure visible, as espoused by French architect and theorist Eugène Viollet-le-Duc—with his emphasis on "sinewy" architecture to achieve a lighter structure—and some of the "organic" designs by US skyscraper pioneer Louis Sullivan. Among the most distinguished architectural examples of the style is Victor Horta's Tassel House (1893), Brussels, Belgium.

3-SECOND BIOGRAPHIES
VICTOR HORTA
1861–1947
Belgian designer and key European Art Nouveau architect

HENRY VAN DE VELDE
1863–1957
Belgian painter, architect, and pioneer of Art Nouveau style

HECTOR GUIMARD
1867–1942
French practitioner of Art Nouveau, whose works include the entrances to the Paris Metro

30-SECOND TEXT
Dragana Cebzan Antic

Curvaceous forms were inspired by different configurations of plants in Art Nouveau.

INTERNATIONAL STYLE

the 30-second architecture

The International Style emerged in the late 1920s, during the early decades of Modernist architecture. The term was coined by American art historian Alfred H. Barr, and it derives from an acknowledgment of a common aesthetic preference for rational or functional architectural design, as well as from the book *International Architecture* (1925) by Walter Gropius. Barr characterized the style as emphasizing the volume of the space (space being enclosed by thin planes or surfaces) and not mass and solidity, regularity and not symmetry, a reduction of ornament, use of high-quality materials, fine proportion, and a radical simplification of form. The style can be also defined by its adoption of glass, steel, and concrete as materials of choice. Contributions to this design philosophy are also in its acceptance of industrialized mass-production techniques, the transparency of buildings, and the genuine expression of structure. The ideals of the International Style can be expressed in the slogans that marked this architectural period: "ornament is a crime," "form follows function," "truth to materials," and Le Corbusier's statement that a house is a "machine for living."

3-SECOND FOUNDATION
"International Style" is the term used to describe a style of Modernist architecture that flourished across the world in the early 20th century.

3-MINUTE ELEVATION
In 1932 Alfred H. Barr, Henry-Russell Hitchcock, and Philip Johnson organized a seminal exhibition at the Museum of Modern Art in New York, in which American architects and the public at large could see examples of architectural developments in Germany, France, Belgium, and Holland, as well as the abstract rationalism of De Stijl. One outcome of this was the influential book *The International Style* by Hitchcock and Johnson, which contained works of exhibited architects.

RELATED TOPICS
See also
FORM FOLLOWS FUNCTION
page 78

LESS IS MORE
page 82

3-SECOND BIOGRAPHIES
LUDWIG MIES VAN DER ROHE
1886–1969
German-American architect, one of the pioneers of modern architecture

WALTER GROPIUS
1883–1969
German architect and founder of the Bauhaus School

30-SECOND TEXT
Dragana Cebzan Antic

"International style," was a term coined by Hitchcock and Johnson to elaborate emerging European modern architecture, later used in a broader context to include the ubiquitous glass box buildings.

ART DECO

the 30-second architecture

The name "Art Deco" to describe the prevailing style of the 1920s and 1930s derived from the 1925 Exposition Internationale des Arts Décoratifs et Industriels Modernes held in Paris. However, it was a retrospective term—Hilary Gelson coined it in *The Times* (London) in 1966 to describe the resurgence of interest in it at that time, and it was further popularized following the 1968 publication of *Art Deco of the 20s and 30s* by Bevis Hillier. Designers and architects working in the style—characterized by nonfunctional decorative details, "sunburst" patterns, and expressive and energetic motifs—saw in it a vision of a pleasurable world, decadent even, unspoiled by war and human hardship. It featured symmetrical, geometric, and angular architectural compositions. Its architects and designers were influenced by cultures that made use of geometrical styles, including Japanese, Mayan, and Aztec. Hollywood popularized it—movies featured Deco-styled movie sets and elaborate costumes to reflect the industry's vibrancy and modernity—and gave it truly international appeal. World War II and the austerity of its aftermath brought an end to Art Deco, although it enjoyed a brief revival in the 1980s.

3-SECOND FOUNDATION
Art Deco is a style in architecture and design defined by geometrical shapes, symmetrical design, and stylized natural forms that emerged in the 1920s and 1930s.

3-MINUTE ELEVATION
Art Deco used state-of-the-art materials (including aluminum, glass, stainless steel, chrome, and the new plastics) and motif repetition to achieve simplicity of form. Its aesthetic attributes were in marked contrast to the asymmetrical and curvilinear Art Nouveau style, but, along with Art Nouveau, Art Deco was frequently criticized and even despised by Modernists, who deemed it "decadent" because of its dependence upon decoration and ornamentation.

RELATED TOPICS
See also
AVANT-GARDE
page 106

MODERNISM
page 108

ART NOUVEAU
page 128

INTERNATIONAL STYLE
page 130

3-SECOND BIOGRAPHIES
WILLIAM VAN ALEN
1883–1954
American architect, and designer of the Chrysler Building, New York

SHREVE, LAMB & HARMON
American architectural firm that designed the Empire State Building, New York

30-SECOND TEXT
Dragana Cebzan Antic

Art Deco buildings present a reaction to the reduction of ornamentation in Modernist buildings.

BRUTALISM

the 30-second architecture

The New Brutalism was an architectural movement that sprang out of the ideas of the Independent Group, a young faction who would meet at the Institute of Contemporary Arts in London in the early 1950s. The main architectural protagonists, Alison and Peter Smithson, were searching for a new ethic and aesthetic for the reconstruction of a welfare-state Britain. They were at the center of an avant-garde group at the London County Council architects' department that was inspired by the expressive concrete phase of Le Corbusier. During the postwar austerity years, the most obvious expression of this more "honest" architecture was unfinished materials and exposed services and structure. Fueled by the support of the main British architectural magazines, *Architectural Design* and *Architectural Review*, the New Brutalism became the standard style for the most ambitious local government reconstruction projects in British cities such as Sheffield, Coventry, and London, but also found keen interpretations in the USA, Holland, and Japan. As an avant-garde movement, Brutalism was over by the time Reyner Banham wrote its history in 1966, but as a style it continued well into the 1970s, finding one of its most enduring images in Boston's City Hall, completed in 1969.

RELATED TOPICS
See also
AVANT-GARDE
page 106

MODERNISM
page 108

3-SECOND FOUNDATION
Despite its name, Brutalist architecture has nothing to do with brutality, but is derived from the French *brut*, meaning "raw" or "unrefined."

3-MINUTE ELEVATION
Brutalist architecture is often used as a derogatory term and is associated with poor-quality 1960s concrete housing and shopping centers. However, it was employed successfully for a wide variety of architectural solutions from civic centers to cultural and university buildings. As well as the use of raw materials such as in-situ concrete and exposed brick, Brutalism's other key characteristics are asymmetrical, sculptural forms and the separation of vehicular and pedestrian circulation.

3-SECOND BIOGRAPHIES
ALISON & PETER SMITHSON
1928–93 & 1923–2003
British architects, members of the postwar Independent Group and founding members of Team X

SIR DENYS LASDUN
1914–2001
British architect most famous for London's National Theatre

PAUL RUDOLPH
1918–1997
American architect, former Dean of Yale School of Architecture

30-SECOND TEXT
Steve Parnell

Boston City Hall exemplifies Brutalist architecture, using exposed concrete for its structure and monumental, but sculptural, aesthetic.

April 26, 1917
Born in Guangzhou (Canton), China

1934
Emigrated to the U.S.

1946
Master of Architecture at Harvard Graduate School of Design

1948–55
Director of Architecture at Webb & Knapp, a real-estate development company

1952–4
Awarded a Traveling Scholarship from Harvard and visited France, Italy, and Greece

1955–66
Founding Partner of I. M. Pei and Associates

1956
The Mile High Center, Denver, Colorado, became his first major independent commission

1961
Designed the Mesa Laboratory for the National Center for Atmospheric Research in Boulder, Colorado

1968–78
Worked on the East Building of the National Art Gallery, Washington, DC

1979
John F. Kennedy Library and Museum, Boston, completed

1979
Awarded the American Institute of Architects Gold Medal, the highest architectural honor in the U.S.

1981–9
The Glass Pyramid, Louvre, Paris, Phases I and II, constructed

1982
Designed the Fragrant Hill Hotel, Beijing, China

1983
Awarded the Pritzker Architecture Prize

1989
Designed the Bank of China, Hong Kong

1989
Designed the Morton H. Myerson Symphony Center, Dallas, Texas

1993
Designed the Four Seasons Hotel, New York

1995
Designed the Rock and Roll Hall of Fame, Cleveland, Ohio

1997
Designed the Miho Museum, Shigaraki, Kyoto, Japan

2001–9
Worked on the Macao Science Center, Macao, China

I. M. PEI

Ieoh Ming Pei is one of the great
Modernist architects of public and civic spaces.
His work creates spaces where people can
move around unimpeded and integrate, learn
and create: libraries, museums, art galleries,
council buildings, medical centers, sports halls,
educational buildings, research buildings,
concert halls, corporate offices, and banks.
His work can be seen all over the U.S., as well
as in India, China, Japan, and Europe.

Born in China, the son of a banker, Pei arrived
in the U.S. at 18 to study Architecture at the
University of Pennsylvania. Unimpressed by
the old-school teaching, he transferred to
Massachusetts Institute of Technology to
study Architectural Engineering. At the same
time he discovered Le Corbusier's work and
his architectural theory. At MIT Pei was
encouraged to return to architecture studies,
which he did but retained in his approach a
successful integration of functioning structure
and aesthetic, engineering, and art. Pei's ideas
were reinforced by his mentor at Harvard
Graduate School of Design, Walter Gropius,
and by the early 1950s his signature style—a
more humane form of Modernism—was
established. His preferred materials are glass,
concrete, stone, wood, and steel, and his
designs are based on clean lines and timeless
geometric forms, the whole seamlessly and
harmoniously blending into its surroundings.
Pei believes that architecture should mirror
nature and is unafraid to express himself in
large buildings erected for the pleasure and use
of many—for example, he was one of the first
architects to use the glazed atrium and the
piazza to provide a modern solution to the
articulation of large public spaces.

His talents have attracted influential patrons.
Jacqueline Kennedy Onassis chose his design
for the John F. Kennedy Library and Museum in
Boston, and the then French President François
Mitterrand commissioned Pei to provide one
of the most controversial of his Grands Projets,
an intervention at the Louvre. In both instances
Pei's design more than rose to the occasion,
the Louvre in particular. His timeless glass-
pyramid design is an elegant solution that
works for the museum's existing buildings
and the people who use them and is now an
iconic site of Paris.

Pei's architectural genius and influence has
not gone unrecognized. He is the recipient
of almost every architectural honor there is,
including the illustrious Pritzker Prize, and
is still working today in his 90s.

FUTURE

FUTURE
GLOSSARY

Adaptive Reuse Alternative name for Creative Reuse, in which, rather than being demolished, a building is reused by being converted from one purpose to another.

BedZED Beddington Zero Energy Development is a housing development in southwest London, opened in 2003, that was designed to be environmentally friendly. The aim was for each resident to have an eco footprint of 1.0 planet (neutral), and this was to be achieved through, among other factors, use of low embodied-energy building materials, water and energy efficiency, and encouraging ownership of LPG vehicles and providing charging points for electric cars. Resident satisfaction is high, although green targets have not been reached with each person causing a footprint of 1.7 planets, which, while around half the UK average, is not neutral.

BIM Building-information modeling, a type of CAD for managing a whole building project through the creation of a three-dimensional model to a fourth dimension, time, and a fifth, cost. In this way, every aspect of a building project can be managed and outcomes predicted. Any changes that occur during construction can be easily factored in and will be reflected in the way the overall model accommodates this.

bioclimatic architecture Refers to the design of buildings based on local climate conditions, aimed at providing thermal, acoustic, and visual comfort, utilizing solar energy and other environmental sources. The basic elements of bioclimatic design are passive solar systems which are incorporated onto buildings and use such natural sources as the sun, air, wind, water, soil, and vegetation to heat, cool, and illuminate buildings.

biomimicry Alternative term for biomimetics—biomimesis and bionics are others—in which models from the natural world provide the template for manmade materials and machinery.

biomorphism The use of human or animal forms in architecture. One example is Félix Candela and Santiago Calatrava's L'Hemisfèric in Valencia, Spain (1998), which is shaped to resemble a giant eye—appropriately, as it houses a planetarium, laserium, and IMAX cinema.

CAM Computer-aided manufacturing, where CAD software is used to design, then control and direct the manufacture of components and tools.

CNC Computer-numerical-control software is used for the operation and management of tools, often employed by architects and designers to create three-dimensional models of designs.

embodied energy Term used to describe the total resources and energy spent in producing an object. In architecture, the embodied energy of any building project can be calculated—and, for eco-friendly projects, be offset over time by built-in efficiencies and green planning for transport and other services.

Gaia hypothesis Also called the Gaia theory, this was put forward in the 1960s by British scientist and environmentalist James Lovelock. It proposes that the Earth's biosphere is a single organism formed by a complex interacting system comprised of all organic and nonorganic material contained within it.

greenwashing A green form of whitewash, the term was first used in 1986 by American environmentalist Jay Westervelt to describe PR and marketing that attempted to exploit the public's eco sensibilities with erroneous or exaggerated green claims for a given product.

in silico Phrase used to describe simulations or experiments done on a computer "in silicon"—the cyber counterpart to *in vivo*, which refers to experiments done on living organisms.

rapid-prototyping printers Printers that create three-dimensional models from data output from CAD programs.

solid-modeling software Programs that create extremely accurate three-dimensional images, inside and out, so that surface elements can be peeled away and the inside viewed.

thermocuring photopolymers Polymer used to create three-dimensional printed models that can be heat-cured.

three-dimensional additive layering A form of three-dimensional printing in which a model is made up from very thin layers, some as fine as 0.00197 in.

CAD

the 30-second architecture

The use of computers for design purposes originates in the aerospace and automotive industries of the 1960s. The development of software and applications expanded 20 years later when computers became more affordable, and early solid-modeling packages from that period are still used—CATIA (1981, Dassault Systèmes) and AutoCAD (1982, Autodesk), for instance. Today, design-and-engineering practice is unthinkable without CAD and CAM (computer-aided manufacturing) technologies, and architecture students are thus required to be proficient in several CAD applications—including parametric modeling, scripting, and programming—as well as BIM (building-information modeling). BIM responds to the increasingly complex workflows and data management involved in building construction by producing a bespoke, comprehensive, three-dimensional representation of the design as parametric and shared objects. These can be accessed and amended by the professionals involved (architects, surveyors, engineers, contractors). Since the objects are defined by parameters and are related to other objects, local changes will affect the global attributes with instant feedback on emerging construction and costing problems.

3-SECOND FOUNDATION
CAD (computer-aided design) refers to the use of computer systems in the process of drafting, creating, modeling, analyzing, simulating, and optimizing a technical design.

3-MINUTE ELEVATION
CAD software packages are ubiquitous in the design and engineering professions. They are implemented for 2D-drafting and painting, 3D-modeling and rendering, and 4D- simulations and animations. Output can be electronic files for visualization, print, or fabrication by CAM programs, and CNC (computer-numerical controlled) machines such as cutters (laser, plasma, water-jet, oxy-fuel), rapid-prototyping printers (using three-dimensional additive layering or thermocuring photopolymers), or industrial robots.

RELATED TOPICS
See also
AVANT-GARDE
page 106

HIGH-TECH
page 116

3-SECOND BIOGRAPHIES
FRANK GEHRY
1929–
American architect and a pioneer of CAD architecture

WILLIAM JOHN MITCHELL
1944–2010
Australian-born architect, and author of *Computer-Aided Architectural Design* (1977)

GREG LYNN
1964–
American architect, known for his CAD design and theory

30-SECOND TEXT
Marjan Colletti

Modern architectural practice is heavily reliant on CAD and 2D- and 3D-drafting software packages.

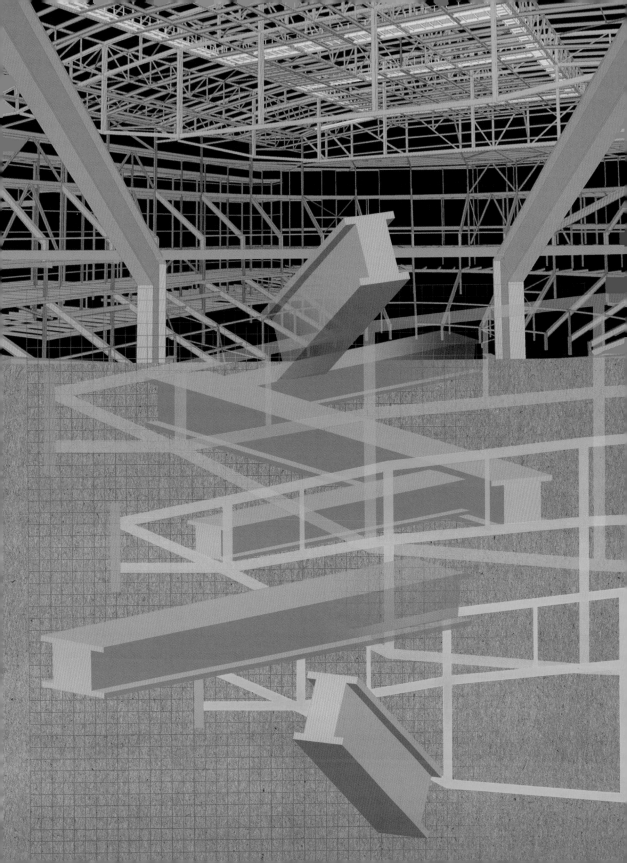

July 23, 1933
Born in Florence, Italy

1962
Graduated from Yale
School of Architecture

1963–7
Set up Team 4 with
Norman Foster, Wendy
Cheeseman, and Su
Brumwell

1964
Designed the conceptual
Zip-Up House

1971
Won commission, with
Renzo Piano, to build the
Pompidou Center in Paris

1977
Founded the Richard
Rogers Partnership

1980–2
The Inmos Building,
Newport, Wales, built

1979–84
Worked on the Lloyd's
Building, London

1989
Designed the European
Court of Human Rights,
Strasbourg

1993–2001
Worked on 88 Wood
Street, London

1998
Invited by the British
Government to set up the
Urban Task Force to
investigate and offer
solutions to urban
decline in Britain

1999
Worked on the Millennium
Dome, London

2001–8
Worked on London branch
of Maggie's Centre

2005
Madrid-Barajas Airport
Terminal 4 opened

2006
National Assembly for
Wales, Cardiff,
completed

2006
Chosen as architect of
Tower 3 for the new World
Trade Center, New York

2007
Awarded the Pritzker
Architecture Prize

2007
Set up Rogers Stirk
Harbour + Partners

2007
Worked on One Hyde
Park, London

2008
London Heathrow Airport
Terminal 5 completed

2012
Completion of Neo
Bankside development,
London

RICHARD ROGERS

Lord Rogers is regarded as the coinstigator and promoter of the High-tech style of architecture along with his former partner Sir Norman Foster, Sir Michael Hopkins, Sir Nicholas Grimshaw, Santiago Calatrava, and Renzo Piano. High tech—a radical take on late Modernism—eschews the Classical tradition and embraces the technological future, expressing itself through an industrial aesthetic using steel and prefabricated elements and, in Rogers's hands, bright primary colors on key elements, injecting a bit of fun into the functional.

After early, mainly conceptual, work on prefabricated housing—the Zip-Up house (1964), for example—Rogers received wider public attention in 1971 when, together with Renzo Piano, he won the commission to design the Pompidou Center in Paris. They delivered a radical "inside-out building," featuring service ducts and staircases on the outside and leaving the interior space uncluttered for exhibitions and crowd circulation. Although extremely influential, the new style was not without its critics, some of whom referred to it as "Bowellism" because of the intestinal pipework that snaked over the buildings.

Rogers went on to build the iconic Lloyd's Building in London, a building that, in being uncluttered by the trappings of architectural custom, bears a strong resemblance to the Italian Futurist Antonio Sant'Elia's 1914 vision of a modern city. Throughout the 1980s and 1990s his partnership concentrated on public buildings, museums, airport terminals, large-scale housing blocks, and industrial premises such as the Inmos Microprocessor Factory in Newport, Wales—a marriage of High-tech aesthetic with high-tech purpose and a model of what architectural historian Reyner Banham has called the "serviced sheds."

One of his better-known designs that unwittingly courted controversy was the Millennium Dome in London (1999), a huge and rather elegant tent that was tainted by the badly received exhibition it housed—although Rogers's Dome itself has since been successfully used to house the O2 Arena for concerts along with other event spaces.

Despite his sometimes controversial approach, Rogers is popular with architects and the general public. He has received almost every award for architecture, including the Pritzker Prize, and is one of the few architects familiar to those outside the profession. Latterly, Rogers has concentrated on tackling the problems of urban decline, becoming advisor to two mayors of London and contributing to urban policies in Shanghai, Paris, Barcelona, and New York. Knighted in 1981, he was created a life peer in 1996, Lord Rogers of Riverside.

CREATIVE REUSE

the 30-second architecture

It is often simpler and probably cheaper to demolish a building and construct a replacement than it is to reinvent or "reprogram" an existing structure. However, for a building to which a certain cultural value is attached (such as a heritage listing, particular aesthetic properties, or its function as part of a familiar skyline), it may be more appropriate to modify rather than replace it. This can involve a mix of approaches, spanning restoration, conservation, reconstruction, the insertion of new services, radical structural interventions, or the design of an interior that shelters within the "envelope" of the original building. The conversion of London's Bankside Power Station into Tate Modern is an internationally acclaimed example of the practice of creative reuse, as it embodies significant spatial changes to a structure that was conceived for entirely different purposes. The reworking of Germany's Thyssen Steelworks as a public leisure space is a bold example of such practices. Creatively reused buildings often contain the traces of previous functions, for example, form, volume, materiality, and unique (usually redundant) features such as chimneys or industrial fixtures. Rather than working against the new use, however, these can often enhance it.

RELATED TOPICS
See also
AESTHETICS
page 86

HISTORICISM
page 88

SUSTAINABLE ARCHITECTURE
page 150

3-SECOND FOUNDATION
Creative reuse—or adaptive reuse—describes the conversion of a building from one function to another, subverting the maxim "form follows function."

3-MINUTE ELEVATION
Creative reuse is now commonplace, especially in countries undergoing industrial and social change. Awareness of "embodied energy"—where buildings have outlived their original purpose, but for which the "energy investment" of constructing them has been met—means that recycling buildings is a sustainable act, as well as preserving architectural heritage. Architects often wrestle with the question of whether to make their changes permanent or reversible. Some buildings resist reuse, however, due to complexity and cost.

3-SECOND BIOGRAPHIES
CARLO SCARPA
1906–78
Italian architect who remodeled the Castelvecchio Museum, Verona, Italy

HERZOG & DE MEURON
1978–
Swiss architectural partners, designers of Tate Modern, London, UK

LATZ & PARTNER
1968–
German architects, known for landscaping the Thyssen Steelworks, Germany

30-SECOND TEXT
David Littlefield

Creative reuse adapts buildings by designing in uses not conceived during the original design process.

BIOMIMETICS

the 30-second architecture

From Native American tepees,
Egyptian lotus, papyrus, or palm columns, to
Greek Corinthian ornamentation, architecture
has always looked to nature for inspiration.
Beyond the zoomorphic and phytomorphic
formal imitation of organic architecture,
biomimetics looks closely at how evolutionary
processes have optimized living organisms over
billions of years to adapt efficiently to their
environments. It evaluates manufacturing,
organizational, and mechanism strategies on
various levels (organism, behavior, ecosystem),
and thus is seen as one of the most promising
emerging principles in sustainable 21st-century
design. Since the 19th century, among the most
notable architects inspired by nature are Alvar
Aalto, Santiago Calatrava, Buckminster Fuller,
Antoni Gaudí, Bruce Goff, Hugo Häring, Imre
Makovecz, Frei Paul Otto, Eero Saarinen, Rudolf
Steiner, and Frank Lloyd Wright. In recent
decades, starting with Janine M. Benyus
(*Biomimicry: Innovation Inspired by Nature*,
1997) then Steven Vogel and Julian Vincent in
the 2000s—but due mostly to the advances of
computation and digital fabrication—biomimetic
principles are being simulated *in silico* with
increasing precision, pushing the boundaries
of computational form generation, material
engineering, and environmental performance.

3-SECOND FOUNDATION
Biomimetics is the
study, distillation, and
development of the
structure, form, formation,
or structure of biological
systems and materials as
models for design.

3-MINUTE ELEVATION
The term "biomimetics" is
rooted in the Greek words
for "life" and "imitation."
It was first coined in the
1950s by American
biophysicist and polymath
Otto Schmitt, and it is
often used synonymously
with biomimicry,
biomimesis, and bionics.
Besides the most famous
example of biomimetics,
Velcro (in imitation of the
burrs of the burdock
plant), is the recent and
award- winning kinetic
façade of the Al Bahar
Towers by Aedas (2012)
in Abu Dhabi.

RELATED TOPICS
See also
ORGANIC ARCHITECTURE
page 110

HIGH-TECH
page 116

ART NOUVEAU
page 128

CAD
page 142

3-SECOND BIOGRAPHIES
FREI PAUL OTTO
1925–
German architect, engineer,
and authority on biomorphic
lightweight structures

JOHN FRAZER
1945–
British architect and CAD pioneer

30-SECOND TEXT
Marjan Colletti

Like a protective skin,
fiberglass mesh parasols
on the façade of the Al
Bahar Towers open and
close in response to the
movement of the sun,
reducing heat and glare.

SUSTAINABLE ARCHITECTURE

the 30-second architecture

3-SECOND FOUNDATION
The concept behind sustainable architecture is that our architectural-design decisions today should not negatively impact on the health, opportunities, or prosperity of future generations.

3-MINUTE ELEVATION
While environmental considerations dominate the discourse, ideas on sustainability have developed to include other areas—economic and social concerns in particular. Precise definitions of sustainability are difficult to agree on, resulting in the term being used for political or economic gain, a technique known as "greenwashing." However, one thing is certain: in the developed world buildings are responsible for using a significant proportion of the planet's finite resources.

Sustainable architecture emerged in the late 1960s with counterculture's criticism of Modernism's tenet that technology could solve any problem. The 1973 oil crisis was the first sign that a fossil-fuel-free future was essential, and sustainable architecture became linked with an awareness of finite resources. It has evolved to encompass several narratives, not least the threat of global warming. Architectural design responded with green architecture, which incorporates several key strategies. First, reducing energy consumption, which in colder climates essentially means using passive solar heating and conserving heat by improved insulation and using heat exchangers; in warmer climates, the emphasis is on excluding heat and using passive ventilation to reduce dependency on air conditioning. Second, adopting carbon-free energy generation for electricity and heating—such as photovoltaic panels and wind turbines. Third, using natural, replaceable, or recyclable materials, and taking account of the "embodied energy" of building components as well as their extraction, transport, production, and eventual disposal or reuse. Ken Yeang's bioclimatically designed building, Menara Mesiniaga (1992), in Subang Jaya Selangor, Malaysia is a high-profile example of sustainable architecture.

RELATED TOPICS
See also
MODERNISM
page 108

ORGANIC ARCHITECTURE
page 110

CREATIVE REUSE
page 146

BIOMIMETICS
page 148

3-SECOND BIOGRAPHIES
JAMES LOVELOCK
1919–
British environmentalist

KEN YEANG
1948–
Malaysian architect, known for designing "green" skyscrapers

30-SECOND TEXT
Steve Parnell

Designed in response to the specific climate of Malaysia, Menara Mesiniaga has in-built passive low-energy features, including solar shading, natural ventilation and lighting.

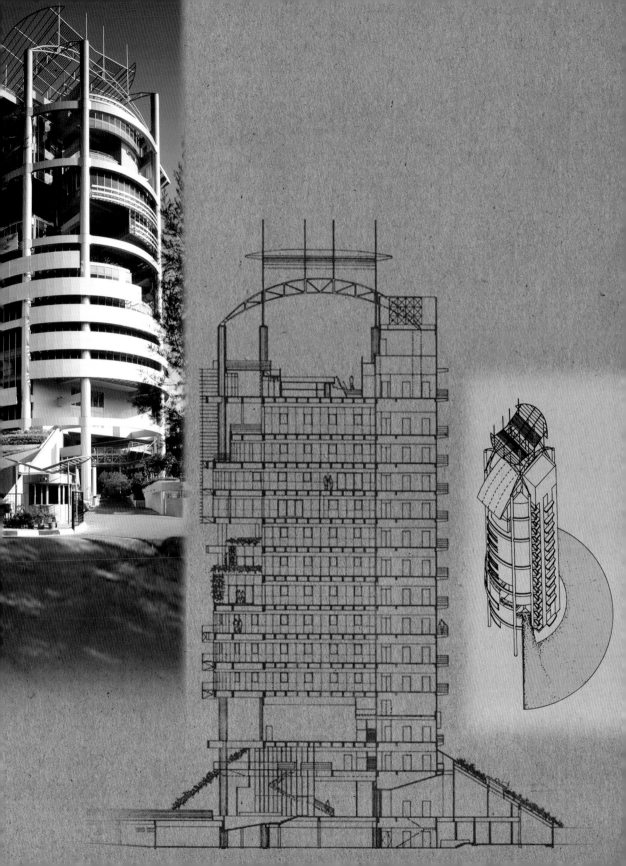

APPENDICES

RESOURCES

Aesthetics and Architecture
Edward Winters
(Continuum, 2007)

Architectural Voices: Listening to Old Buildings
David Littlefield and Saskia Lewis
(Wiley, 2007)

The Arts and Crafts Movement
Elizabeth Cumming and Wendy Kaplan
(Thames & Hudson, 2002)

Atlas of Vernacular Architecture of the World
Marcel Vellinga, Paul Oliver, and Alexander
Bridge
(Routledge, 2007)

Baroque: Architecture, Sculpture, Painting
Rolf Toman
(Ullmann Publishing, 2010)

*Changing Ideals in Modern Architecture
1750–1950*
Peter Collins
(McGill-Queen's Press, 1998)

The Classical Language of Architecture
John Summerson
(Thames & Hudson, 1963)

*Critical Regionalism: Architecture and
Identity in a Globalised World*
Alexander Tzonis and Liane Lefaivre
(Prestel, 2003)

*Designing with Nature: The Ecological Basis
for Architectural Design*
Ken Yeang
(McGraw Hill, 1995)

*Disclosing Horizons: Architecture,
Perspective and Redemptive Space*
Nicholas Temple
(Routledge, 2006)

*From Models to Drawings: Imagination and
Representation in Architecture*
Marco Frascari, Jonathan Hale, and
Bradley Starkey (eds)
(Routledge, 2007)

The Gothic Cathedral
Colin Wilson
(Thames & Hudson, rev. edn, 1992)

Greek Architecture
Arnold Walter Lawrence
(Yale University Press, 5th edn 1996)

High Tech Architecture
Colin Davies
(Rizzoli, 1988)

A History of Western Architecture
David Watkin
(Laurence King, 2005)

*Kenzo Tange and the Metabolist Movement:
Urban Utopias of Modern Japan*
Zhongjie Lin
(Routledge, 2010)

The International Style
Henry-Russell Hitchcock and Philip Johnson
(W.W. Norton & Co., 1997)

The Language of Post-Modern Architecture
Charles Jencks
(Academy Editions, 6th edn 1991)

Minimalist Architecture
Franco Bertoni
(Birkhäuser Architecture, 1998)

Modern Architecture
Alan Colquhoun
(Oxford University Press, 2002)

Modern Architecture: A Critical History
Kenneth Frampton
(Thames & Hudson, 4th edn 2007)

Modern Movements in Architecture
Charles Jencks
(Penguin, rev. edn 1987)

The New Brutalism: Ethic or Aesthetic
Reyner Banham
(Architectural Press, 1966)

On the Art of Building in Ten Books
Leon Battista Alberti
(MIT Press, 1988)

Orientalism
Edward Saïd
(Routledge & Kegan Paul, 1978)

Ornament and Crime: Selected Essays
Adolf Loos
(Ariadne Press, 1998)

Scale: Imagination, Perception and Practice
in Architecture
Gerald Adler, Timothy Brittain-Catlin, and
Gordana Fontana-Giusti
(Routledge, 2012)

The Sphere and the Labyrinth: Avant-Gardes
and Architecture from Piranesi to the 1970s
Manfredo Tafuri
(MIT Press, 1987)

The Story of Post-Modernism: Five Decades
of Ironic, Iconic and Critical in Architecture
Charles Jencks
(John Wiley & Sons, 2011)

The Ten Books on Architecture
Vitruvius
(Dover, 1960)

Theory and Design in the First Machine Age
Reyner Banham
(MIT Press, 1980)

Words and Buildings
Adrian Forty
(Thames & Hudson, 2004)

A World History of Architecture
Marian Moffett, Michael Fazio, and Lawrence
Wodehouse
(Laurence King Publishing, 2004)

NOTES ON CONTRIBUTORS

EDITOR

Edward Denison is an independent consultant, writer, and architectural photographer. His work focuses on sustainability and the built environment. Edward is coauthor of *How to Read Bridges* (2012), and has written over ten books on different aspects of architecture and design around the world. He has a Ph.D. in architectural history from the Bartlett School of Architecture, University College London, where he teaches architectural history and theory.

FOREWORD

Jonathan Glancey is a writer, broadcaster, and architecture and design consultant. He was Architecture and Design correspondent of *The Guardian* from 1997 to 2012 and Architecture and Design Editor of *The Independent* from 1987 to 1997. An Honorary Fellow of the Royal Institute of British Architects, his books include *The Story of Architecture*; *20th Century Architecture*; *Lost Buildings* and *Dymaxion Car: Buckminster Fuller* (with Norman Foster).

Dragana Cebzan Antic is an architect, urban designer, and writer in the field of interactive architecture and design. She regularly contributes to the British and international architectural press and teaches urban design at the Bartlett School of Architecture, University College London.

Nick Beech is an architectural historian, currently teaching at several English universities: the Oxford Brookes University, the University of Westminster, and the Bartlett School of Architecture, University College London.

Marjan Colletti is an architect, architectural educator, researcher, and coprincipal of marcosandmarjan design practice in London. He is Professor and Codirector of the Institute for Experimental Architecture.Hochbau at the University of Innsbruck, Austria, and Senior Lecturer in Architecture at the Bartlett School of Architecture, University College London. He was guest editor of the relaunch issue of *AD: Exuberance* (2010) and has written several books on architecture, of which his latest is *Digital Poetics* (2012).

Anne Hultzsch is an architectural historian specializing in the histories of architectural criticism and visual perception. She teaches at the Bartlett School of Architecture, University College London, where, in 2011, she was also awarded her Ph.D. She is the author of several titles and is currently researching Nikolaus Pevsner's writing in the *Architectural Review* during the 1940s as well as finalizing her latest book, *Architecture, Travellers and Writers: Constructing Histories of Perception 1640–1950* (2013).

David Littlefield is a writer, curator, and teacher of architecture and design with an MA (distinction) in Interior & Spatial Design from Chelsea College of Art & Design, part of the University of the Arts London. He is currently Senior Lecturer in the Department of Planning and Architecture at the University of the West of England in Bath, England.

Steve Parnell is an architect, a historian of modern architecture, and architectural critic. He regularly contributes to the British and international architectural press and is currently Lecturer in Architecture at the University of Nottingham, England.

INDEX

A

Aalto, Alvar 92, 148
Adaptive reuse 140, 146
Adler, Dankmar 84, 85,112, 113
aesthetics 86–87, 124, 146
Alberti, Leon Battista 26, 27, 46, 76, 88, 100
Ancient Egyptian architecture 16–17, 46, 62
Andreu, Paul 38
Anthemius of Tralles 22
anthroposophist philosophy 96, 110
Apollodorus of Damascus 20
arch 12, 13, 20, 24, 28, 34, 35, 36–37, 38, 40, 42, 46, 48
Archigram 90, 106
architrave 12, 18
Aristotle 76
arris 34, 40
Art Deco 16, 123, 126, 132–133
Art Nouveau 85, 96, 110, 123, 128–129, 132, 148
Arts & Crafts 14, 75, 82, 104–105, 110, 128
Avant-garde 50, 78, 82, 90, 106–107, 108, 114, 132, 134, 142
axonometric projection 66–67

B

Banham, Reyner 134, 145
Baroque architecture 27, 36, 38, 40, 96, 97, 98, 100, 102, 123, 124–125
Bauhaus 74, 106, 108
beam 12, 13, 18, 38, 42–43, 46, 50
Beaux Arts 98
Bernini, Giovanni Lorenzo 124
BIM (building information modeling) 140, 142
bioclimatic architecture 140
biomimetics 14, 110, 140, 148–149, 150
Blondel, Jacques-François 56
Borromini, Francesco 124
Boullée, Étienne-Louis 90
Brunelleschi, Filippo 38, 100
Brutalism 134–135
Burke, Edmund 75, 86
Burlington, Earl of 45, 62
Buscheto di Giovanni Giudice 24
buttress 12, 28, 36, 40, 48–49
Byzantine architecture 13, 22–23, 24, 30

C

CAD (computer-aided design) 58, 60, 68, 116, 140, 141, 142–143, 148

Calatrava, Santiago 36, 140, 145, 148
CAM (computer-aided manufacturing) 140, 142
Candela, Félix 40, 140
caryatid 34, 46
catenary arch 34, 35, 36
central plan 12, 22, 30
Chambers, Sir William 126
chinoiserie 122, 123, 126
Choisy, Auguste 66
Classical Greek architecture 12, 13, 16, 18–19, 20, 22, 28, 36, 46, 56, 62, 70, 76, 88, 98, 102
Classicism 46, 88, 96, 97, 98–99, 100, 124
CNC (computer numerical control) 141, 142
Cockerell, Samuel Pepys 126
coffering 34
column 12, 13, 18, 20, 24, 34, 36, 42, 46–47, 48, 50, 98
compound dome 34, 38
Constructivism 74, 82, 106, 108
Creative reuse 140, 146–147, 150
Critical regionalism 14, 92–94, 118
Cubism 97, 108
cutaway drawing 54, 66

D

da Vinci, Leonardo 26, 27, 54, 55, 64, 68
Deconstructivism 96, 118
De Stijl 106, 108, 130
dome 13, 20, 22, 24, 30, 34, 35, 36, 38–39, 40, 50
Dürer, Albrecht 58, 64

E

elevation 58, 60–62, 68
embodied energy 140–1, 146, 150
English Baroque 96, 98
Enlightenment 122, 124
entablature 12, 13
Escher, M. C. 80
Euclid 64, 76
Evans, Robin 56, 60
exploded-view drawing 54, 66
Expressionism 96

F

fan vault 34, 40
Fibonacci 54
numbers 54, 68
figure–ground diagrams 74, 80
flying buttress 12, 28, 36, 48
Foster, Sir Norman 116, 144, 145
"Form follows function" 78, 104, 108, 130, 146

frame 12, 34, 42, 48, 50
Frampton, Kenneth 92
Frazer, John 148
Fuller, Buckminster 90, 110, 148
Functionalism 74, 78, 96
Futurism 96, 106

G

Gaia hypothesis 141, 150
Gaudí, Antonio 35, 36, 96, 123, 124, 148
Gehry, Frank 62, 96, 142
geodesic dome 34, 38
Gestalt psychology 74, 80
Gibberd, Frederick 80
Gilpin, William 86
Goff, Bruce 110, 148
golden ratio 54, 68, 76
Gothic architecture 12, 22, 24, 28–29, 30, 34, 36, 40, 48, 56, 62, 102, 104
Gothic Revival 88, 102, 122
Graves, Michael 118
Greek Revival 88, 98, 102
Greene, Charles and Henry 104, 126
greenwashing 141, 150
Grimshaw, Sir Nicholas 38, 145
groin 12, 24
Gropius, Walter 71, 82, 108, 130, 137
Guimard, Hector 110, 128

H

Häring, Hugo 110, 148
Hawksmoor, Nicholas 96, 102, 124
Heidenreich, Erhard 28
Hejduk, John 60
High-tech 38, 116–117, 142, 145, 148
Historicism 75, 88–89, 102, 146
Horta, Victor 128
human scale 54, 68

I

Ictinus 18
Independent Group 74, 122, 134
inflexed arch 34, 36
informatics 96
International Style 78, 108, 130–131, 132
Isidore of Miletus 22
Islamic architecture 30–31
isometry 66

J

Japonism 122, 123, 126
Jeanneret, Pierre 70, 71
Jefferson, Thomas 45, 102
Jencks, Charles 118
Jenney, William Le Baron 50, 84
Johnson, Philip 75, 118, 130
Jones, Inigo 45, 55, 62
Jugendstil 123, 128

K

Kahn, Louis I. 40
Kant, Immanuel 86
Kurokawa, Kisho 114

L

Lahauri, Ustad Ahmad 30
Lasdun, Sir Denys 134
Latz & Partner 146
Le Corbusier 46, 54, 56, 68, 70–71, 76, 97, 108, 116, 130, 134, 137
Ledoux, Claude-Nicolas 98, 102
"Less is more" 50, 74, 82–83, 130
Lethaby, William R. 104
Libeskind, Daniel 62, 96
Loos, Adolf 55, 58, 78, 82
Lovelock, James 141, 150
Lynn, Greg 142

M

Makovecz, Imre 110, 148
Mannerism 97, 98, 124
Metabolism 106, 114–115
Meyer, Hannes 56
Michelangelo 100, 124
Mies van der Rohe, Ludwig 35, 46, 50, 71, 74, 82, 130
Minimalism 74, 82
Mitchell, William John 142
Modernism 35, 42, 46, 58, 66, 75, 78, 82, 88, 92, 96, 106–109, 114, 116, 118, 122, 126, 128, 130–134, 145, 150
Modernism 123, 128
Modulor system 54, 68, 70, 71, 76
Morris, William 104
Murcutt, Glenn 92

N

Nash, John 126
Neo-avant-garde 106
Neoclassicism 27, 55, 62, 75, 90, 98, 102
Nervi, Pier Luigi 38
New Brutalism 74, 92, 106, 123, 134
New Urbanism 97, 114, 118
Niemeyer, Oscar 82
oculus 13, 20
orders (classical) 12, 13, 18, 20, 27, 98

O

Organic architecture 14, 110–111, 112, 128, 148, 150
Orientalism 122, 123, 126–127
orthographic drawing 54, 58, 60
Otto, Frei Paul 148
Ozenfant, Amédée 70, 97

P

Palladio 44–45, 55, 62, 98, 100, 102
Paper architecture 90–91
Paxton, Sir Joseph 40

Pei, I. M. 136–137
pendentive 13, 22
perspective 60, 64–66
Piano, Renzo 50, 116, 144, 145
picturesque 74, 86
pier 13, 22, 24, 36, 46
piloti 35, 46
Piranesi, Giovanni Battista 90
plan 56–57, 58, 60, 62, 66, 68, 80
postcolonial theory 126
Postmodernism 46, 75, 88, 92, 108, 116, 118–119
Prairie School 75, 78, 112, 113
Primitive/Vernacular 14–16
pronaos 13, 20
proportion 68, 76–77, 86
Pugin, A. W. N. 88, 102
Purism 97, 108

R
Rationalism 108
Raumplan 55, 58
Renaissance 27, 38, 40, 54, 55, 56, 60, 62, 64, 66, 74, 76, 88, 97, 98, 100–102, 124

Revivalism 16, 75, 88, 102–103, 123
Rococo 98, 124
Rogers, Richard 12, 50, 116, 144–145
Roman architecture 12, 13, 16, 18, 20–21, 22, 24, 28, 30, 36, 38, 40, 46, 62, 76, 88, 98, 102, 124
Romanesque architecture 22, 24–25, 28, 30, 36, 40, 48
Romanticism 74, 88
Rowe, Colin 76, 80
Rudolph, Paul 134

S
Saarinen, Eero 36, 148
Sant'Elia, Antonio 106, 145
scale 56, 58, 60, 64, 66, 68–69, 76
Scarpa, Carlo 146
Scott Brown, Denise 118
section 56, 58–59, 60, 66, 68
Sinan, Mimar 30
Smithson, Alison and Peter

122, 134
Soane, Sir John 102
solid-modeling software 141, 142
solid–void 80–81
springer 34, 35, 36
Steiner, Rudolf 96, 110, 148
Stile Floreale 123, 128
Stirling, James 118
stoa 13, 18
Structuralists 123
Sullivan, Louis 78, 84–85, 110, 112, 113, 128
sustainable architecture 146, 150–151
symmetry 62–63, 86

T
Tange, Kenzo 114
Tatlin, Vladimir 106
Team X 123, 134
trabeated 13, 18, 20

U/V
Unités d'Habitation 70, 71, 97, 108
Utopian 75, 90

Utzon, Jørn 92, 110
Van Alen, William 132
Van de Velde, Henry 128
Van Doesburg, Theo 66
vanishing point 55, 64
vault 12, 13, 20, 24, 28, 34, 35, 36, 38, 40–41
Venturi, Robert 118
Viollet-le-Duc, Eugène 48, 128
"Vitruvian Man" 27, 54, 55, 68, 76
Vitruvius 13, 14, 20, 26–27, 45, 46, 54, 55, 60, 75, 76, 78, 88, 98
voussoir 35, 36

W
Wren, Sir Christopher 45, 96, 98, 124
Wright, Frank Lloyd 75, 78, 90, 110, 112–13, 122, 126, 148

Y
Yeang, Ken 150

ACKNOWLEDGMENTS

PICTURE CREDITS
The publisher would like to thank the following individuals and organization for their kind permission to reproduce their images in this book. Every effort has been made to acknowledge the pictures. However, we apologize if there are any omissions.

Sergei Arssenev: 107BR; Stefan Bauer: 99BR; Peter Bronski: 133C; Canam Group Inc: 143; Erik Christensen: 93; Corbis/Paul Almasy: 70 /Christopher Felver: 136; Edward Denison/Aedas (2012): 149; Andrew Dunn/ www.andrewdunnphoto.com: 67T; Fotolia: 44; Axel Kuhlmann: 89C; Library of Congress, Washington D.C.: 59T, 112, 133L, 133TR, 133R; Stephen Montgomery: 89T; Steve Morgan: 199B; Tom O'Connor: 105R; Clemens Pfeiffer: 129T; Rex Features/Nils Jorgensen: 144; David Shankbone: 199T; Cédric Thévenet: 92T; Ken Yeang/ © T.R. Hamzah & Yeang Sdn. Bhd. (2012): 151